Just Call Me Janie
The Unlikely Story of the First Woman Elected to Alabama's Supreme Court

Conversations with
Janie Shores

JUST CALL ME JANIE

An Intellect Publishing Book

Copyright 2016 Janie Shores

ISBN: 978-1-945190-00-1

Cover design and artwork by Michael Ilacqua
www.cyber-theorist.com

Editor, Illustrator
Anne Kent Rush
www.annekentrush.com/

Proofreader
Ellie Lockett

First Edition: April 30, 2016
FC-23H

All rights reserved. No part of this book may be reproduced in any form or by any electronic, mechanical, or other means now known or hereafter invented, including photocopying or recording, or stored in any information storage or retrieval systems without the express written permission of the publisher, except for newspaper, magazine, or other reviewers who wish to quote brief passages in connection with a review.
Please respect Authors' Rights.

Visit the website: www.JanieShores.com

Intellect Publishing, LLC
6581 County Road 32, Suite 1744
Point Clear, AL 36564
www.IntellectPublishing.com
Inquiries to: info@IntellectPublishing.com

JANIE SHORES

*This book is dedicated
to
Laura and Verla*

JUST CALL ME JANIE

CONTENTS

FOREWORD: VINCENT FONDE KILBORN III
INTERVIEWER'S NOTE: ARDEN SCHELL

SECTION ONE: ROOTS

"We hold these truths to be self-evident, that all men are created equal, that they are endowed by their Creator with certain unalienable Rights, that among these are Life, Liberty and the Pursuit of Happiness. That to secure these Rights, Governments are instituted among Men, deriving their just powers from the consent of the governed."

U. S. Declaration of Independence, 1776

INTERVIEW I - 2/10/2010: **FROM POTATOES TO PROFESSOR**
PAGE 5

INTERVIEW II - 2/16/2010: **A DOG NAMED DEMOCRAT**
PAGE 61

INTERVIEW III-11/29/2010: **PARENTS, PATRONS, & PREJUDICE**
PAGE 81

SECTION TWO: RIGHTS

"A State Supreme Court's responsibility is to correct errors of lower courts, deciding cases based solely on U.S. law, regardless of the personal politics and preferences of the judges."

USlegal.com

INTERVIEW IV – 12/5/2010: **FROM JANIE'S SUMMARIES TO THE SUPREME COURT**
>PAGE 127

INTERVIEW V– 12/12/2010: **COFFEE WITH BEAR BRYANT; CAKE WITH MORRIS DEES**
>PAGE 149

INTERVIEW VI – 1/11/2011: **A JUDGE'S WORK IS NEVER DONE**
>PAGE 167

SECTION THREE: REFORMS
"In all criminal prosecutions, the accused shall enjoy the right to a speedy and public trial, by an impartial jury…"
>U.S. Constitution, Bill of Rights, Amendment VI

INTERVIEW VII – 1/19/2011: **JUSTICE IS TRIAL BY JURY**
>PAGE 199

INTERVIEW VIII – 2/2/2011: **SHE NEVER LOST A CASE**
>PAGE 213

REFERENCES
>PAGE 239

POSTSCRIPT
EXPANDED CONTENTS
BOOKS & OTHER MEDIA
LETTER FROM THE WHITE HOUSE
PUBLISHER'S NOTE
A DISSENTING OPINION
ACKNOWLEDGEMENT

JANIE SHORES

"In my judgment, the name Janie Ledlow Shores should be inscribed, along with Helen Keller and Julia Strudwick Tutwiler, at the top of the list of Alabama's Greatest Women."

Senator Howell Heflin

FOREWORD

I have known Janie Shores since I was about 10 years old. Although I have two wonderful younger sisters, Mary Joe Brierly (whom I call Sissy) and Margaurite Kilborn (whom I call Baby Sis), I always thought of Janie as my older sister.

My father was Vincent Fonde Kilborn, Jr. He was an outstanding, talented, and well-respected lawyer with a thriving law practice in Mobile, Alabama, a lawyer's lawyer. His most prestigious client was Archbishop Thomas J. Toolen, himself a legend for establishing a strong Catholic diocese and educational system in Alabama.

Janie began working for Daddy as a legal secretary in the early 1950s. One of her talents was perfect shorthand. Daddy dictated letters and pleadings to her, usually on Saturday mornings. Janie could write as fast as Dad could talk – no small feat. This shorthand skill was to serve her well later in law school.

She took verbatim notes of what the law professors said in class. Janie's typed notes were so good that she was once accused of cheating when she wrote exam answers in a professor's exact words. Her notes were later sold by the Alabama School of Law Book Store and titled "Janie's Summaries." I used these summaries myself in law school.

Over time, Daddy recognized Janie's keen sense of the law. One day, while he was dictating to her on the subject of future interests (an archaic subject few lawyers understand), he suggested she consider getting a college degree and then going on to law school. She took his suggestion.

In those days, it was almost unheard of for women to go to college, and even more so for a woman to become a lawyer. Janie later told me that such a thought had never crossed her mind until Daddy suggested it that day. His recognition of that spark of legal genius launched her into a storied legal career.

After Janie left Daddy's law firm to go to college and get her law degree from the University of Alabama, I didn't see her as much except when she would visit our home on Bienville Avenue in Mobile. But, when she did visit, something occurred that sticks with me even today.

I remember sitting in the living room listening to spirited legal debates between Daddy and Janie. It was like watching a tennis match. Janie, still wet behind the ears from law school, seemed to more than hold her own in these legal debates. She was the only person I ever saw who seemed to be able to occasionally best Daddy.

Her visits were always fun occasions for this teenager. Both of them seemed to enjoy the give and take of the conversation immensely. Always adding to the ambiance were cold gin martinis with a twist of lemon. That clear magic fluid in those martinis enlivened the proceedings and made the laughter louder when somebody scored a point.

As Janie was graduating from the University of Alabama Law School, they had a job fair at the law school. It was always attended by many prestigious law firms wanting to hire the brightest and best students.

One day Janie saw a sign advertising the fair. While she was reading it, Dean Harrison, a wonderful teacher himself, matter-of-factly commented to her that the job fair was really "not for you." He explained that law firms would not be interested in hiring a woman lawyer. Dean Harrison was not trying to be mean, but simply telling her how it was. Intuitively, she had already accepted this and did not protest.

Eventually, Janie got a job working as general counsel for Liberty National Insurance Company. Later, with the urging and approval of influential friends, clients and, of course, Mr. Kilborn, she ran for a six-year term on the Alabama Supreme Court and was elected as the first woman on the Alabama Supreme Court.

Janie got re-elected for three more terms. Indeed, I believe she was the first woman in the nation to be elected to a state supreme court. Others before her were appointed, but not elected.

Janie also helped start Cumberland Law School and taught there for many years.

Through hard work and unwavering perseverance, immense legal talent, and the ability to write and speak with biting clarity, she became a heroine to aspiring women lawyers in Alabama and the rest of the nation.

She is the perfect example of how a young woman growing up in a little country town, Loxley, Alabama, picking potatoes for pennies, could through courage and perseverance attain the highest levels in the legal profession.

Janie's various positions, including Justice of the Alabama Supreme Court and a Cumberland Law School professor, were the perfect platform for her battle against prejudice and racism. She never shied away from controversy, or wavered from her deeply held principles.

Her stand against racism ultimately ended her marriage to Mr. Ellzey when she refused to join the White Citizens Council of Selma despite the insistence of her father-in-law.

During Janie's time on the Alabama Supreme Court from 1972 – 1995, she wrote 1,300 opinions under her own name and many more *per curiam* opinions for the court. It is hard to fathom the ability to analyze and write on so many and varied legal matters.

Today, Janie enjoys the same wonderful insight, sense of humor, and quick wit that served her legal career well and that her friends and many of her foes always admired.

Probably the best description I can give of her genius is: I have never heard her speak one wasted word or one unclear sentence. Like they used to say in the E. F. Hutton ads, "When Janie Shores talks, everybody listens."

The book that follows is an intimate, honest, and engaging account of Janie's life in her own words. Janie still calls me by my nickname "Sonny," and she still plays a significant role in my life . . . keeping me out of "mischief."

Except for Janie's good friend Mary Joe Kilborn, who also happens to be my mother, Janie Shores remains the most remarkable woman I have ever known.

Sonny

VINCENT FONDE KILBORN III

JANIE SHORES

INTERVIEWER'S NOTE

Janie - what fun. And, how was I so lucky as to be asked to interview Janie for an oral history project of the ABA?

Janie was asked by the American Bar Association to find someone to interview her – preferably a woman lawyer and someone who did not know her. Well, that would be nearly impossible for an Alabama judicial celebrity. However, I was new to the area, did not know Janie or her reputation, and fortuitously was recently introduced to her. The rest was happenstance – she asked, I happily accepted, and we planned our endeavor. Having purchased the appropriate gear, we set out.

I would arrive at Janie's house, set up the recorder and just talk – asking questions, commenting, cajoling, laughing and having a relaxed good time. We would start out on a topic (childhood, law school, jobs, campaigns, etc.) and just let it go where it might.

Janie made it easy. She was so accessible. Not stuffy, like, OMG, I'm interviewing an Alabama Supreme Court Justice! In fact, we would finish a session, late afternoon, and Janie would ask, "Want a drink?" The first time, as always, I said, "Sure." She would pour her "good whiskey," on the rocks, no water, no soda – fine Scotch.

The hardest part of the process was to get Janie to talk about her accomplishments. She would downplay her importance. Specific cases that were particularly noteworthy she would avoid discussing. Always a big-picture person, Janie would focus instead on her participation, as though part of a team. I felt as though Janie did not feel that what she had done was at all exceptional. But it was.

Most importantly, one should focus on her intense determination. Once an idea had been planted, Janie carried through to the end; I think that applied throughout her life.

I was most impressed with the story of her becoming a lawyer.

Searching the want ads after taking a bus to Mobile almost immediately after her high school graduation, she was sent by an agency to a sole practitioner, one of the few offices open on a Saturday. Hired on the spot, she began taking dictation of pleadings and correspondence, which she continued to do for a number of years. During a session of dictation, she took issue with something he said, and after contemplating her remark, he commented that she had a mind for the law. The seed was planted. She had to go to college first.

So she did, taking courses at the nearest university center, accumulating credits. Even after marrying a young man from Selma, she continued her education, sometimes in the face of adversity – moving to Selma, in-laws, work, divorce, travelling to Tuscaloosa. Nothing would stand in the way of her becoming a lawyer. Everything took a back seat. Tenacious is a word to describe Janie.

Remarkable is another. As much as she may demur.

Reading her history will take you on an adventure – a real-life adventure.

Janie spent twenty-four years as an Alabama Supreme Court Justice. She is admired to this day. Her story certainly stands out as a beautiful example for women and young girls everywhere, not just in Alabama. But more than this, Janie is a beautiful person – interesting, caring, and accessible.

As she would say, "Just call me Janie."

Arden Schell

JANIE SHORES

Just Call Me Janie
The Unlikely Story of the First Woman Elected to Alabama's Supreme Court

JUST CALL ME JANIE

SECTION ONE

ROOTS

JUST CALL ME JANIE

JANIE SHORES

ROOTS

"WE HOLD THESE TRUTHS TO BE SELF-EVIDENT, THAT ALL MEN ARE CREATED EQUAL, THAT THEY ARE ENDOWED BY THEIR CREATOR WITH CERTAIN UNALIENABLE RIGHTS, THAT AMONG THESE ARE LIFE, LIBERTY, AND THE PURSUIT OF HAPPINESS, THAT TO SECURE THESE RIGHTS, GOVERNMENTS ARE INSTITUTED AMONG MEN, DERIVING THEIR JUST POWERS FROM THE CONSENT OF THE GOVERNED."

U.S. DECLARATION OF INDEPENDENCE, 1776

CONTENTS

INTERVIEW I - 2/10/2010: **FROM POTATOES TO PROFESSOR**
PAGE 5

INTERVIEW II - 2/16/2010: **A DOG NAMED DEMOCRAT**
PAGE 61

INTERVIEW III - 11/29/2010: **PARENTS, PATRONS, & PREJUDICE**
PAGE 81

PHOTOS
PAGE 117

JUST CALL ME JANIE

INTERVIEW I

FROM POTATOES TO PROFESSOR

Arden: Janie, what can you tell me about growing up in Alabama?

Janie: I was born in Butler County on April the 30th, 1932. My mother remarked on every birthday that English dogwood was in full bloom on the day I was born. English dogwood is beautiful; and she said that always, as if it were very important that I know, that it bloomed on my birthday every year.

Once I asked her, "Did you see the dogwood from the windows in the hospital room?" "Honey, we didn't go to the hospital to have babies back then. Nobody went to the hospital." She was at home.

I was delivered by a Dr. Moorer. It was a difficult birth, resulting in nerve damage in the form of a condition known as dystocia, or Erb's palsy, that causes partial paralysis. In my case, it resulted in impairment of the right arm and shoulder.

I cannot turn my right hand with the palm up, can't put on a jacket or anything else, unless I start with the right side because my arm will not extend back or up enough to get it on after I have put the left side in. I can't use a fork with my right hand, etc. But all these actions I do instinctively now, compensating without thinking about it.

Most people don't notice any impairment now. I simply become left-handed in any activity requiring full right arm mobility. For example, I am a left-handed tennis player; I bat left-handed; can't drive a golf ball at all (but can putt); I eat with my left hand, but write with my right hand. I simply used my left side when the right side didn't work and learned to do so without thinking about it. I do all this without conscious effort and never considered the condition a serious handicap.

A year and a half after I was born, on December 11, 1933, my sister Verla arrived, also at home.

Franklin Roosevelt became president a few weeks before I was born. He died when I was in the 9th grade. When I heard he had died in Warm Springs, Georgia, in 1945, I thought it was the end of the world. Everyone we knew admired him. I can remember exactly where I was when I heard the news. I was on the porch swing in the house we lived in during World War II.

Of course, like everybody else, I also remember exactly where I was when news came that President John Kennedy had been shot and killed in Dallas, Texas, in 1963. I was in the car driving from Gadsden to Birmingham.

I was 20 years old when General Eisenhower was elected president. I was too young to vote, the right to vote was not extended to 18-year-olds until much later. I was for Stevenson, although most everyone I knew was for Eisenhower. I am certain that no member of my family ever voted for a Republican.

Prior to the 1960s Democratic President's support of integration and the Civil Rights movement, being a Democrat or a so-called "Roosevelt Democrat," was pretty basic to being a Southerner. This is because most Southerners felt that in the 1930s, President Franklin D. Roosevelt saved the South and the country. After the devastation of the Great Depression, Roosevelt's New Deal programs restored the country's economy. In the 1940s, my family and most everybody in our area didn't know any Republicans. We had heard about them.

Being so near the same age, my sister and I were almost like twins. In fact, the entire family was very near in age. My mother was 17 years older than I was, and my father was 18 years older than I was. In a sense, all four of us grew up together.

My earliest memories are of playing outside with our cousins. Depending upon the time of the year, we played softball, hide and seek, hopscotch, marbles.

Uncle Hollis, my father's brother was our leader because he was a year or so older than the oldest cousins. He determined what we did on a day-to-day basis. Under his direction we built forts, tree houses, and lots of bird traps. He was very good at it, too. He caught all kinds of birds in those traps. I suspect that I could build a bird trap now.

Both sets of grandparents lived within walking distance of where we lived. My maternal grandfather was Vamon Scott, a first-generation Scots-Irish immigrant. He was a big man with blue eyes and red hair. He and Annie, my mother's stepmother, lived on a farm and raised cotton, hogs, cows, tomatoes, velvet beans.

I remember playing in piles of cotton that were stacked on the porch, called the gallery, before the cotton was hauled away on wagons to the gin in Georgiana for processing. Tomatoes were stored in a dark room to ripen before they were canned. They smelled wonderful.

It was a rural life, no nearby neighbors, never-ending chores, but quite beautiful. It was in many ways a very pleasant childhood. We picked berries: huckleberries, blackberries, chinquapins, and wild pansies. I don't recall being bored or lonely.

Everybody went to town on Saturday. When we were older, we went with our cousins to the movies on Saturday afternoons. We didn't have a car. My paternal grandfather Steve Ledlow, a second-generation immigrant from England (there is a town in England called Ledlow, which is how our name is spelled), had the only car in the family. Sometimes, but not often, the children were allowed to ride with him on trips to town.

Periodically a van called the "rolling store" came by our house. I assume it served as a source for anything one needed before the weekly trip to town. It was a van or truck and sold a few staples such as coffee, sugar, and patent medicines.

I remember we used to wait for it with anticipation although I don't recall that we ever got any treats from the rolling store. I do remember getting some kind of tonic once a year. I don't know what purpose it was supposed to serve but every child was required to take it once a year. The full treatment involved castor oil. The rolling store was very convenient. Wish we still had rolling stores.

Arden: Would you tell me about your grandparents?

Janie: I was closer to, or at least saw more of, my father's parents than my mother's. Their names were Steve and Gertrude Ledlow, or Miss Trudy as my mother called her. We children called them Papa and Granny.

Papa was a tall, thin, handsome man, reserved and mean, I always thought. He seemed to like Verla more than he liked any of my cousins or me. I know she liked him more than I did. He was always dressed in a business suit. All of the grandchildren were in awe of him or afraid of him or both.

In addition to farming cotton, potatoes, and sugar cane, Papa harvested cypress trees and made cypress shingles which he sold for roofing and houses. Cypress is indigenous to our part of the South. The wood is very durable and used to be used extensively. He didn't talk much, or least not to the children.

I remember a big machine in the back of the house called the cane mill. It consisted of two big vertical steel rollers that were turned by a horse attached to a long pole. Sugar cane was fed into it, and juice came out.

Our Aunt Wynona, just a few years older than we were, got her hand caught in the rollers. She bears the scar to this day. She is now in her 80s, lives on the Warrior River near Tuscaloosa, and still goes fishing nearly every day.

Granny talked a lot. She taught us her moral values and her ideas about religion. They used to say she went to church every time it opened. I think that's one of the reasons none of her six children were ardent churchgoers. She must have been a Methodist since she named my father, her first-born son, John Wesley. He never considered himself a Methodist, apparently.

When John was about to go off to World War II, he told me and Verla that if we decided to go to church, to pick out one close to home, that God didn't care what kind it was. And we did. We sometimes went to the Methodist, Baptist, or Presbyterian.

In my own case, I remember an incredibly handsome young priest, Father Claude St. Germaine, a French-Canadian, who was sent by Bishop Toolen to the local parish and half of the young girls in the county, including me, suddenly developed an interest in the Catholic Church.

Arden: Was this in Butler County?

Janie: We were born in Butler County, but we moved to Baldwin County when Verla and I were both in grade school. I was in the third grade, Verla in the second.

Verla and I were pretty close growing up, but we sometimes had disagreements, not serious ones, but we fought sometimes. She was clever; I think she could make her nose bleed at will. We'd be having a fight; Willie and John were about to catch us; and she could make her nose bleed so it would appear that I hit her.

Either one of us would go to the wall for the other one. If somebody else were mistreating me, I could count on Verla to help me, and I would do the same if someone mistreated her. Our relationship didn't require a daily sharing of secrets.

The town in Butler County where we were born was Georgiana, which is about 50 miles south of Montgomery, on Highway 31, which was the main road running north and south in Alabama until the interstate system was built in the late fifties, early sixties. Georgiana was and is a little town. The county seat is Greenville.

Loxley, the little town where we later went to school in Baldwin County, was a beehive of activity in the shipping season. Verla and I rode our bicycles to school. We had a mutual friend named Joanne Holley who lived between our house and school. We used to stop and wait for her to go with us. Life developed into routines with everybody always working. There was seldom a period when there wasn't something to be done, and we all did it.

When Verla grew up, she worked with a banker who started the First Federal Savings and Loan in Mobile. Verla had a very successful career with that institution. She got to be a vice president and made friends who remain her friends to this day.

Arden: Tell me about your father.

Janie: He, like his father, was tall, thin, very proud, very handsome. Neither he nor my mother was very demonstrative. Neither of them talked very much. Neither of them had any education beyond grade school, but both had good minds; and John particularly was a lifelong voracious reader, mostly non-fiction.

Pearl Harbor 1941

Japan bombed Hawaii's Pearl Harbor on December 7, 1941. I remember the teacher showing us Japan and Pearl Harbor on the world map, and that was all everybody talked about. Even the children understood that something profound had happened.

In our case, it meant that John would have to go into the military and he could either wait to be drafted or he could join. He decided to volunteer for the Navy before being drafted. I remember hearing John and Willie discuss this. They agreed that he should enlist so that he'd have a choice of what branch to go into.

They made plans to get us settled before he had to leave. That's when they decided to move down to Baldwin County on the Gulf coast, about 115 miles south of Georgiana. John got a job in the shipyards in Mobile, was building ships as fast as possible for the war. He worked on the second shift as an electrician in the shipyards before going away to a Navy training facility in Great Lakes, Illinois.

After training, he was sent out to the Pacific to the Philippines. I think his group built runways for the upcoming invasion. He spent the war in the Pacific as a member of the Seabees.

We seldom got letters from him, but in one letter, he asked us to send cigarette lighters. Before the war, cheap Zippo lighters were available everywhere, but we were unable to find any kind anywhere during the war. Finally, we found an expensive silver lighter ($20 plus) at a jewelry store in Mobile. Willie reluctantly agreed that we should buy it.

While John was in the service, we lived in Loxley, a little town in Baldwin County about 15 miles east of Mobile. The shipyard was located on Mobile River, east of the city and the ship channel in the bay. John's drive to work was about 30 minutes. He went back and forth to work until he shipped out.

Baldwin County is bounded on the west by Mobile Bay and on the south by the Gulf of Mexico. Most people we knew lived on working farms. Many also worked on shrimp boats or other seafood related businesses. The nearby town of Bon Secour was and is a shrimp and oyster center.

Loxley is located in farming country. The railroad ran down the center of town joining the whole county from Bay Minette in the north to Foley in the south. The railroad was a lifeline enabling farmers to ship the potatoes to market directly out of the fields. Soybeans and corn were grown also on a grand scale. For a time, tobacco and gladiolas were grown in the area for commercial trade.

Auburn University, then known as Alabama Polytechnic Institute, grew all kinds of different plants experimentally at its facility located between the towns of Fairhope and Silverhill. Over the years, it cultivated different varieties of oranges. Orange Beach, now a thriving community on the Gulf of Mexico, was named for the citrus grown there for a time. Satsumas were proven to be hardy there, and many farms still grow them today. Over the years, the University has grown pecans, crepe myrtle, live oaks and recently I noticed a patch of banana trees.

There were lots of cattle farms, and we had a lively cattle auction facility in Robertsdale.

Potato Picking

After John went into the military, Willie worked in a restaurant, and Verla and I worked in the potato industry, first in the fields, and later in the shed. Most of our classmates also worked in the fields.

Potatoes were a big crop in Baldwin County. Our house was next to a potato farm owned by Floyd Marshall. He had moved to Baldwin County from Indiana and established a small farm near Loxley. He and his wife Edna and daughter Ikey were our closest neighbors. He grew red potatoes for a national market. His farm was small, but there were several big farmers in the county.

The Bertolla farm and the Corte farm, owned and operated by Italian immigrants, were among the biggest. These farms, at that time, raised potatoes, corn, peanuts. Big business. Crops shipped out on refrigerated train cars during the season. It's probably wrong to call them refrigerated train cars. They were train cars with ice in them.

Potatoes were planted in late January or early February and were ready for harvest in early spring. Harvesting was well underway by April. The school year was adjusted so that the children could help with the harvest in the potato season. Most of our classmates worked in the fields during the harvest.

Verla and I picked up potatoes for Mr. Marshall. You were paid by the basket. I don't remember exactly how much you were paid for each basket, but it was pennies. I was soon selected to keep track of each worker's production. I kept up with how many baskets all the others picked up and I didn't have to work quite as hard as the others.

Arden: Did you get extra pay for that?

Janie: No, I didn't get extra pay, but it was easier work.

Arden: Where in Baldwin County did you live then?

Janie: Loxley. We rode our bicycles to school. We had a car, but Willie didn't drive it any more than was absolutely necessary. Gasoline was rationed, and tires were irreplaceable.

Almost everything was rationed. One had to have ration stamps to buy a great many things. You had to have stamps to get gas, sugar, and shoes. We used to trade stamps with people to buy liquor and we'd get some stamps for special things we wanted to buy. People didn't use their cars unless they had to because gas was scarce and everybody's cars were getting older. Then there weren't any new cars being built.

Arden: What was it like being a girl during that time? Were you treated differently than how the boys were treated?

Janie: Actually, I don't remember much difference. We all worked in the fields; we did whatever there was to be done. I don't think I knew any classmate who didn't work at something after school. We first worked picking up potatoes in the fields. When we got a little older, we worked in the potato shed.

The potatoes were unloaded from trucks into a machine that washed them and, as they went tumbling through, divided them into sizes, and rolled them down a conveyor belt. People along the line threw out any defective ones. The machine moved them pretty fast, so you had to be attentive to pick all of the defective ones out before they flowed into sacks. The sacks were sewn up by hand before being put on train cars and shipped off to market.

I know that after a while working on the line, I was allowed to sew up the sacks. I don't know whether I was paid any more than the line workers. I doubt it. I think everybody was paid the minimum wage that was probably forty cents an hour.

I didn't know exactly where the market was but I had heard that the commodities market was in Chicago, and I knew that it was important to get our potatoes to market to beat some other market further north. Activity in Loxley, Robertsdale, Summerdale, and Foley picked up significantly during harvest time.

We didn't have a Western Union in Loxley at most times of the year, but during potato harvest Western Union would set up an office in Loxley, and the traders, men in ties with Yankee accents, would be in town for the season. It was real commerce, and there was excitement in the air.

It made a strong impression on me. I thought it was significant that the interest in the harvest in Baldwin County, Alabama, was such that Chicago dealers would come here to watch the market.

The sheds were owned and operated by either of two Italian immigrant families. In Loxley, it was the Bertolla family. The Corte family was big in the county, too. I think that family owned the sheds in Robertsdale, maybe Foley, too. Albert, Ferdinand, Ernest, and Forrest Corte are names I remember. The Bertollas had a sister named Viola who made an impression on me. She worked in the office, and I remember that she was a Notary Public.

I didn't know exactly what that was, but I remember that her signature was required to get a birth certificate for me and that my birth certificate was necessary in some way in connection with John going into the Navy. I am pretty sure that Verla had to have a delayed birth certificate, too.

I assume that to be automatically registered one needed to be born in a hospital. Neither of us was, so Willie had to get witnesses who could swear that we were born to John and Willie, when and where, and their statements had to be notarized. Viola Bertolla was the only notary in Loxley.

When we weren't working on the shed, all three of us—my mother, sister and I all worked in a restaurant. In Loxley, there was only one restaurant. It was owned by Floyd Lovell and was run by Gladys, his hard-working second wife. Gladys did all of the cooking and supervised every other activity.

The restaurant was pretty busy, particularly during shipping season and during the summer. It was located on Highway 59, the only road to Gulf Shores, and although there were very few permanent people who lived there, summer visitors increased business for everybody. We not only had all the out-of-towners here for the potato harvest, traffic increased with more people coming to the beach.

There weren't many motels or hotels on the beach. A few people, mostly from Mobile, had summerhouses. There were no condominiums, no high-rises of any sort. It was just pristine open beach, and we went with regularity when we weren't working and when we could get a ride.

I shouldn't have gone, and Verla shouldn't have either. I had fair skin and freckles. Verla had darker hair, but both of us would just burn up in the merciless sun. I was always putting vinegar on myself to treat the awful sunburn that we got. I don't recall that it helped much, but someone told us that it did. My mother sewed little thin cotton jackets for us to wear in the fields to shield us from the sun. They helped a little bit..

A Woman Named Willie

Arden: Tell me more about your mother.
Janie: She was the youngest in her family. I don't know exactly how many brothers and sisters she had but I know that her mother died when she was an infant, and she had at least two sisters and several older brothers. She was raised by her stepmother whom we called Annie.

My mother was always referred to as "Willie." Only when she died did we discover her real name was Wilhelmina. She hated the name and didn't tell anybody what it really was. Everyone called her Willie.

She was resourceful, too, and had strict rules that we were required to follow. We had to have a hot breakfast every day, which meant no bought cereal. We might have oatmeal sometimes, but mostly breakfast meant either bacon or ham and eggs, with grits and homemade biscuits that she made every morning. That was just the rule.

My parents taught us that there is a clear distinction between right and wrong. We were raised to be respectful and law-abiding. These teachings served me well in later life with moral issues in the community and in the law.

I don't remember my parents specifically discussing prejudice or telling us not to be racist, but they taught us to be honest and fair. If we all are supposed to treat others as we want to be treated, then prejudice and unequal policies are unacceptable. When you know right from wrong, you don't hesitate when moral choices have to be made.

As I was saying about working, everybody worked, all the time. After the war started and community activity increased, Willie became the local telephone operator for Gulf Telephone Company that was owned by the Snook family who came here from Indiana, I think.

That same telephone company still operates in the county, but the Snook family sold it a few years ago. It's limited to Foley, Robertsdale, Summerdale, Loxley, Gulf Shores, and Orange Beach. Even today you have to call long distance from other towns in Baldwin County to those towns.

John Snook, not the patriarch, but the only son of the founder, was famous around here for training the women who worked for him during the war to do everything involved in maintaining the company while the men were at war. My mother was in the telephone office, so she wasn't among them, but many women strung lines and installed and repaired telephone equipment and did all of the things that there were no men left home to do.

Looking for Spies

We were told that John Snook sincerely believed that there were German submarines in the Gulf during World War II. I don't know whether there really were or not, but he and a lot of other people were very concerned about that. It would be a good place for an enemy to come to shore because the area was pretty deserted and at that time, there were few people living there. The Snook family sold the telephone company many years later. John's widow has supported many philanthropic projects in the county.

One of our jobs after school during those years was identifying airplanes. After school, we would walk to the telephone office where my mother worked and search the skies for airplanes. I don't know how official it was, but we were given little booklets with the planes' sketches showing the outlines of planes. We were to identify any that we spotted by marking those little sketches. I remember seeing what I thought looked like the little sketch of the B-52 that we were given. I assumed that this vigil was something civilians could do to help the war effort.

Arden: How old were you then?

Janie: Maybe 12 or 13. We went to school in Loxley through the ninth grade. Then we had to go to Robertsdale to go to school. It was six miles south of Loxley, so we wouldn't have been able to walk to the telephone office after school, as we did in those earlier school years.

A school bus came for us and took us to Robertsdale High School. It was what was called a consolidated high school, where students from schools in Loxley, Rosinton, Silverhill, and other little communities were sent for high school.

We had high schools in Robertsdale, Foley, Bay Minette, and Fairhope. I think those were the only high schools we had at that time. Students from surrounding communities that had grade schools went to the consolidated schools.

Arden: What kind of student were you?

Janie: I made good grades, but I don't think I was too challenged. The best teacher I had was Mrs. Hiles who taught English. She taught the usual classics and required us to memorize a certain number of poems each week. I'd type them. All of the girls and some boys took typing. I would type the poem to be memorized on a piece of paper so I wouldn't have to carry around the book while I was committing the poem to memory.

Once Mrs. Hiles caught Harold, the boy sitting behind me, reading a poem off of my paper as he was standing up to recite it. After class, she accosted us both and required us both to repeat the poem right there. I had no problem reciting it, but Harold stumbled a time or two. Mrs. Hiles required him to recite it in class again the next day.

One of our friends was telling a group about the incident and started by asking, "Did you hear what that bitch did to Harold?" just as Mrs. Hiles walked up. Without missing a beat, she continued "And I don't blame her." All of us thought that was the fastest we had ever known Louise to think.

Arden: What else did you participate in at school?

Janie: Well, we had girls' softball teams and competed with other schools. We were very serious about it. We also played volleyball. From time to time, we would get up a neighborhood tennis game. A group of girls sometimes sang at assemblies, but it was not a formal choir, just a group of us who apparently felt moved to sing every once in a while.

The boys had, of course, football, baseball, and basketball. I was most active in softball. I played first base and was a pretty good left-handed hitter.

And everybody worked. During the year, after school was out, you had a job and in the summertime you had a job.

My brother Larry was born in 1948, one of the World War II baby boomers. Willie went back to work pretty soon after he was born, and Verla and I came home early from school to look after Larry for the last couple of years we were in high school.

A Bus to a New Life

I graduated from high school on a Friday in April 1950. The next day, Saturday, I caught the Greyhound bus and went to Mobile. I looked in the phone book and found an employment office within walking distance of the bus station, walked to it and pronounced that I was looking for a job. I could take shorthand and I could type.

An attractive woman took my application and said, "Well, of course, most places are not open on Saturday," but she looked in her files and found one that indicated that Saturday interviews were being conducted.

She sent me for an interview with Vincent F. Kilborn, Jr., a lawyer then practicing alone, having only recently returned from serving in World War II. Before the war he had practiced with a legendary Mobile trial lawyer, Harry Seale, who had also been his father's law partner. His father, Vincent F. Kilborn, Sr., had died in a plane crash when his four sons were still young boys.

As it turned out, the Vince Kilborn who gave me my first real job was to have a profound impact on my life. He was the first person to suggest, directly or indirectly, that education beyond high school might be possible for me.

I am sure that our parents expected Verla and me to finish high school, and they would have been disappointed had we not done so, but they never said so. We never considered not finishing high school, although several of our friends and classmates dropped out. A few got married and quit. One got pregnant, quit school, and then got married. Others found full-time jobs and quit. But I don't recall that any of our teachers ever talked about the importance of education beyond high school.

The day after graduating, I was hired as a secretary in the office of Vincent F. Kilborn, Attorney at Law, 307 First National Bank Building, Mobile, Alabama, phone 2-2635. I remember the address and telephone number to this day.

I loved the job and I came to love the wisdom of the common law. I was proud to have even a minor part in it.

Thanks to the training I received at Robertsdale High School, I was proficient in shorthand and typing, the primary tools in that day before the advent of modern computers. We did have electric typewriters, but there were no Xerox machines. We soon acquired a Dictaphone, but Mr. Kilborn didn't like to use it much, and I preferred to take dictation. So for a long time the office was closed to clients on Wednesday afternoons and Saturday mornings, and those times were used for dictation of everything: letters, legal pleadings, deeds, wills, briefs, contracts.

Fortunately, I was good at shorthand and could accurately record everything he said. Over time, I learned to anticipate what he would probably say in a given context.

Janie's Summaries Save the Day

As it turned out, those long hours on the job taking and transcribing legal pleadings and documents were invaluable once I got to law school. I was able to take down every word the professor said in class and later transcribe them. At the end of the semester, I reduced all of these notes to what we called "summaries" of about 30-40 pages. I did this in every class, and they became my only study material for the final exams.

I shared the notes with my friends, and over time *Janie's Summaries* became widely distributed.

Reproducing them was not easy in the 1950s. I sometimes made a carbon copy as I wrote them, maybe two, but otherwise making copies was complicated. There were no Xerox or other copy machines. Photostat copies could be made, but they were expensive and came out with white letters on black paper.

Years later I heard that my summaries were sold to law students at Malone's Book Store, and for years lawyers who came along after I had been long graduated told me how my summaries had saved them in one class or another.

Interestingly, these summaries and these lawyers became very helpful to me when I ran for the court in a statewide race. My name was familiar to lawyers in almost every county, an enormous boost in a statewide election to a first-time candidate.

My experience in Mr. Kilborn's law office on those Wednesday and Saturday dictation sessions was especially invaluable for the procedural courses in law school.

Most law students had never seen legal pleadings, and common law pleading was especially vexing. Mobile retained the common law distinction between law and equity, with common law courts and Chancery courts exercising equity jurisdiction. Distinct methods of pleading existed for each court.

One filed complaints "at law" on the law side and "bills in equity" in the Chancery, or equity side of Circuit Courts. This clear distinction between law and equity was retained in Mobile long after other circuits in the state had abandoned this strict distinction in the pleading stage.

In the Circuit Courts in Mobile, all cases were "plead at length." On the law side, a case was initiated by the filing of a complaint. The legal effect of the complaint was tested by demurrer, which asserted that the complaint failed to state a legal claim. If the demurrer was sustained, the complaint was dismissed, and the plaintiff was required to file an amended complaint that was again tested by demurrer.

A plea in abatement might follow which asserted that although good as a matter of law, the proceeding should be abated for any number of reasons. All of this could take place before defenses on the merits were interposed. There were replications (plaintiff's reply to defendant's plea), rejoinders (a defendant's answer to plaintiff's reply), surrejoinders (a plaintiff's reply to a defendant's rejoinder), etc.

In other parts of the state, either by court rule or accepted practice, all of this had been simplified so that once a complaint had survived a simple motion to dismiss, the case proceeded on answers raising procedural objections as well as defenses on the merits.

In Birmingham and in most of the state outside of Mobile, complaints were answered by a "plea in short by consent," signifying that the parties by agreement dispensed with the burdensome strictures of common law pleading.

While simplified pleading was laudable, there was an elegance to common law pleading which led to a greater understanding of the law under the "case method" utilized in most law schools after having been introduced at Harvard Law School many years ago.

A Mentor Recognizes Talent

Arden: How did Mr. Kilborn treat you?

Janie: Kindly, but he expected perfection and promptness. I'd take dictation for at least four hours, and it would take three or four days to transcribe it all.

I was very fond of him and have been forever grateful to him for making me understand that I could make of my life whatever I had the will to do. He was the first person to ever make that clear to me.

He was extremely bright; it seemed to me, exceptionally so. He could dictate all of those things without reference to anything, just out of his head, and they were elaborately complicated, many of them. That impressed me, of course.

One day, when I was taking dictation, I commented on the substance of whatever the subject was, I'm not sure exactly what, and he looked at me and said, "I need to tell you this. I think you have an uncanny feel for the law. You ought to go to law school."

Mr. Kilborn was a very intelligent man and would not have suggested something that was impossible; so when he casually assumed that I could do that, it was a revelation. It then dawned on me for the first time in my life that it might be possible for me to go to college and even beyond. Up until that time, nobody had ever mentioned college. Even our teachers didn't say to us, "Hope you'll go to college." They just didn't do it. I think because they understood that, well, college just wasn't possible for most of us.

It was a much different time to be in public schools than it is now. Today, everybody's concerned about what college their kids will be going to starting in kindergarten.

Arden: There probably wasn't much money then.

Janie: Oh, no, of course. I'm sure it was sensitivity to that issue that caused the teachers not to dwell on a college future for us. That being true, just about everybody got married pretty soon after graduating from high school and some before.

My friends and I didn't discuss college. We were pretty bright, made the highest grades, and all that, but nobody talked about going to college. Almost all of us assumed it was beyond our reach.

Arden: Once he expressed this thought to you, how did going to college become a possibility?

Janie: Mr. Kilborn's encouragement set me to investigating how to make it happen. I started looking into what the requirements were for going to law school. I found that a college degree was among the things required.

I remember I talked to Vince's brother, Ben, just out of Georgetown Law School in Washington, DC, about the time I was leaving. I said, "Ben, what's the secret to success in law school?" He said, "Honey, you won't have any trouble if you use their own words as often as you can when writing the exams for the professors. They can't disagree with their own words." So that's what I did.

Ben and I remained close friends until the day he died, which was way too early. He died in the early 1970s before I was elected in 1974. He had cancer. He did not live very long after being diagnosed with it. I think by the time he died, too young, all but one of his brothers had also died. There were four boys in the family, and the youngest, Ben, lived the longest, and he died at about age 54.

Today, Vincent Fonde Kilborn, III, the son of the man who gave me my first job, is practicing law here in the Mobile area. I call him Sonny, as did his parents when he was growing up. He lives within walking distance from my house now, about ten minutes down the bay a little bit. He is an outstanding lawyer, as was his father. I think he's amazed to have lived to reach 70, which he's just done. I don't think he ever expected that. All of the men in his family, his father and three uncles, died before they reached sixty years old: three with cancer, and one had a heart attack. Isn't that a shame?

Their father, also named Vincent F. Kilborn, was killed in a plane crash at the airport in Mobile. He was returning from a business trip to Montgomery on a private plane when they were children.

Vince's mother, whose name was Marguerite, was memorable. She was still active when I was working in the law office in the 1950s. She raised those four boys on her own, with a mandatory trip to the Catholic Church every time it opened. I think all of them remained faithful to the Church until they died. I know the oldest one was. As I said, he grew up to represent the Archbishop of the Diocese of Mobile.

When I first worked for Mr. Kilborn, there was a young lawyer in the office, an associate, whose name was Jack Edwards; he later became an outstanding member of Congress. He was elected in what was called "the Goldwater Sweep" in Alabama in 1964. I think every Republican who ran for office in Alabama in 1964 won, while Goldwater lost in the rest of the country.

Jack Edwards ran for Congress as a Republican in the election of 1964 and won. He served for years in Congress and seldom had serious opposition. I was quite fond of him, and he was a good Congressman. He now lives here in Fairhope.

I asked Jack one day, "Jack, how long would it take me to get a law degree if I started right now?" He said, "Well, Janie, it takes four years to get an undergraduate degree and it's going to take another three to get a law degree – that's seven years."

"My question was, if you devoted full time and took the maximum amount of courses, and so on, how much could you reduce that seven years?" "Oh," he said, he wasn't sure, "but who would want to do that?"

Well, that's what I did. I started right away taking courses at the University of Alabama Center in Mobile.

A Young Man from Selma

It was during that same time that I met a young man from Selma, Alabama. He was down here running a small grocery store that his father bought for him. He had attended Auburn but did not graduate. I never did hear the entire story but I think either he or his father, or both, wanted him to do something else before joining his father in the family business in Selma.

My school friend, Louise Tuberville introduced me to him. His name was Bill Ellzey and he was the owner and sole operator of a little grocery store, first in Steelwood, a small community on Highway 59, north of Loxley, and then in Loxley. I had seen him around but didn't know him well. I started dating him and after a few months I met his family.

His parents wanted him to come home to Selma and work in the family business. His father owned and operated a sand and gravel company in Selma and manufactured concrete pipe, all connected to the road-building industry.

His parents were very nice to me. His father kindly told me that Bill suffered from petit mal seizures from time to time. No particular treatment was available that I recall. Bill's father thought it was something that I should know, and it was. I would have been scared to death had I not had some warning.

His parents encouraged us to get married and move to Selma. I was especially fond of his father and got along well with both of them. In addition to Bill, they had a young daughter Marie who was in high school. They were all very welcoming to me when we got married in the summer of 1953. Shortly afterward, Bill and I moved to Selma.

Immediately I got a secretarial job at Craig Air Force Base, Selma, and enrolled in the University of Alabama Center there, taking as many hours as allowed.

Brown v. Board of Education

You know how you remember exactly where you were when significant events happened? For instance, I was sitting in the swing on our porch when I heard that President Roosevelt had died. I remember that I was home in the first apartment Bill and I had in Selma, on Dallas Avenue, when I read the headline in the *Selma Times* announcing the Supreme Court's decision about school desegregation in *Brown v. Board of Education*. That was the summer of 1954. I read the headline and realized that something profound had happened.

Arden: How old were you then?

Janie: I think I was nineteen. I turned eighteen just a day or so before I graduated from high school and I was nineteen when we got married.

I took as many courses as I could get at the University Center in Selma and then went to Judson College, located in Marion, Alabama, about an hour or so from Selma.

Judson College is a Baptist school, girls only. Marion is a little town dominated by Judson College for girls and Marion Institute, a military school for boys.

I drove back and forth from Selma to Marion and took almost two years' worth of work at Judson. Then I transferred to the University of Alabama because by that time I had learned that after completing 90 hours of undergraduate work, you could enter law school. The last 30 of those hours had to be earned on campus, but once completed you could enter law school and get an undergraduate degree at the end of your first year of law school.

Stated differently, this program allowed you to get both an undergraduate degree and a law degree by entering law school after earning 90 semester hours in undergraduate school. You were supposed to apply for the undergraduate degree at the end of the first year of 30 hours in law school. It was like an undergraduate degree with a major in law.

Law School Before College

I met all of the requirements but failed to apply for the undergraduate degree after that first year in law school. I went on to graduate from law school in August 1959.

I would come to regret failing to apply for my undergraduate degree at the end of that first year in law school. It is no excuse, but the truth was, I was preoccupied with final exams in law school that first year and after all, I was there for a law degree from the beginning.

All of those explanations or excuses didn't do me any good in 1967. By that time, I had been admitted to the bar since 1959, and I was teaching law at Cumberland Law School, Samford University, in Birmingham. Cumberland Law School was an old law school that had been located in Lebanon, Tennessee. Cordell Hull, Secretary of State under Roosevelt, and a native of Tennessee, is its most famous alumnus.

Arthur Weeks was responsible for persuading Howard College, a Baptist college in Birmingham, to buy Cumberland and relocate it to Birmingham in about 1962. Weeks had been practicing law in Birmingham when he heard that Cumberland Law School in little Lebanon might be acquired. He persuaded Leslie Wright and the board of directors of Howard College to buy it.

I later asked him what one got when one bought a law school. I think the price was $125,000. He said the most valuable asset was the alumni list, but also included were books, furniture, and portraits of past deans.

First Female Law Professor in the South

Once relocated to Birmingham, Weeks set about hiring a faculty. He first looked to retired military men with law degrees. He then called me and asked if I was interested in joining the faculty he was putting together. I agreed and started teaching there in 1964, becoming the first female law professor, he used to say, in the South.

Money was scarce, and I'm certain that he was trying to assemble a faculty as economically as possible. No doubt this played a part in his calling me. That, plus the fact that I was then on the legal staff of Liberty National Life Insurance Company that was founded by the Samford family, great benefactors of Howard College, later renamed Samford University.

Having acquired Cumberland, Dean Weeks set about assembling a faculty, recruiting more students, and getting the school accredited.

He must have been reviewing all faculty records because he came to my office in 1966 or 1967 and said he didn't have a copy of my undergraduate degree. I assured him that there was no problem; I would simply call the University of Alabama in Tuscaloosa, 50 miles from Birmingham, and have it sent. After all, I had earned it in 1956. Well, the call was unsuccessful. I was told that at least 12 semester hours must be earned on campus in the semester in which the degree is awarded.

Of course, at this time, I was teaching full time at Cumberland, and it would have been difficult to commute to

Tuscaloosa and take 12 hours toward my undergraduate degree while teaching full time in Birmingham.

I pleaded my case all the way to the president's office, then occupied by an acting president because President Rose retired. The acting president was unimpressed with my hardship argument. The result: I transferred my undergraduate credits from Alabama and entered undergraduate school at Samford where I was on the law school faculty.

I earned an AB degree from Samford in 1968, my law school degree having been earned at the University of Alabama in 1959.

Arden: Where did you work when you lived in Selma?

Janie: At Craig Air Force Base in Selma. It's no longer there. I always worked all through my schooling. Bill worked for his father's very successful sand, gravel, and concrete business.

Arden: How did you accomplish getting to your classes in Tuscaloosa while you were working?

Janie: I had to quit my job at Craig Air Force Base when I started full-time courses on the main campus in Tuscaloosa. I went to school full time. I took the maximum number of hours I could, just trying to get enough hours to get into law school.

Arden: Did you still go back and forth every day?

Janie: Not every day. It got to be too much; the work was too hard. It's about an hour's drive, maybe a bit more. I think it was more than that. I'd normally go to Tuscaloosa on Monday morning, maybe come home once during the week, and come back on Friday afternoon.

Arden: How was your pursuit of the law received by your husband, his family, and your family?

Janie: He never complained because it had been understood from the beginning that was what I was going to do. I told him that. I was taking those courses at the University

Center in Mobile when we talked about getting married. On moving to Selma, I did not plan to stop going to school. He said that was all right. It didn't make any difference to me much where I got the undergraduate work. That worked out fine.

Arden: Did anybody, including your family, have any issues about your work?

Janie: My family here? No.

Arden: You were pretty much on your own, right?

Janie: Yes, and had been for some time. The problems started when I was living in Selma but they had nothing to do with my being in school.

Selma Responds to Integration Ruling

The first friction between the Ellzey family and me came in discussions about integration. When *Brown v. Board of Education* was released in 1954, everybody was discussing what that would mean and how it would affect life in Alabama, and in Selma particularly.

The general view was there would be no integration of the schools. Various views were expressed, but it was apparent that it was not going to go smoothly. Some were willing to shut the schools down if necessary. Others were talking about creating private schools for the white children. I don't recall anybody advocating compliance with the legal decision.

Before any serious effort was undertaken to integrate the grammar and high schools, there was a serious effort to integrate the university in 1956. I was transitioning from undergraduate school to law school at the beginning of the second semester. You've got to remember the times. Integration of the schools was a constant topic. People constantly talked about the Supreme Court and the integration decision. I remember thinking, "Oh, Lord, life here is going to change a lot and it's not going to be fun."

They were not overtly racist; by "they" I mean the Ellzeys and the people of Selma. They were very nice to the black people, especially to their own employees, but that didn't mean they were going to let them register to vote. Or go to white schools. And those topics were beginning to dominate all conversations. The subject was really getting controversial.

Autherine Lucy Makes History 1956

Efforts to integrate the University of Alabama were going on during that time. Autherine Lucy tried to register on the Tuscaloosa campus in 1956.

I was in undergraduate school in the fall semester and entered law school in the second semester, 1956. Autherine sought to register at the same time as I was entering law school. There was a lot of talk among the students, but the real protest came from non-students, large groups who came and lined the streets of the campus and made a lot of noise.

The crowds kept getting larger and louder, and the police were everywhere, and after a few days Autherine was gone. The talk was that the threats against her and her family drove her decision. I remember that there were songs made up about her. It was said, and I think it is largely true, that the mobs consisted mostly of white non-students.

In Selma, the conversation about integration was constant, and the determination to resist was evident everywhere. It was clear that this issue was going to come to a head one of these days, sooner rather than later.

In Tuscaloosa, things on campus settled back down after Autherine withdrew. Integration of the University and the schools in general was discussed among the law students, even though there was no debate about it between faculty and students.

The subject of race relations dominated the 1958 governor's campaign. Jim Folsom could not run again. His second term as governor was ending, and there were lots of candidates running to replace him. Among them were George C. Wallace, John Patterson, George Hawkins, and James "Jimmy" Faulkner. Most of the law students were supporting one or another of the candidates.

George Hawkins, president pro tempore of the senate, was considered the liberal among the group, and the rest claimed to be moderate on the race issue, at first, but that became the only issue in the run-off between Patterson and Wallace.

George Wallace the Liberal

John Patterson had the support of the Ku Klux Klan, the KKK, in the run-off with George C. Wallace. Wallace was considered the moderate on the race issue, and Patterson assumed the role of protector of the status quo or no integration of schools. In later years, those two would change roles. Patterson actually supported John Kennedy in the 1960 presidential race and was responsible for the Democrat getting at least some of the Alabama electoral votes.

Gerald "Sag" Wallace, George's younger (not much) brother, was in law school at the time. He was older than the average law student, having been in the military before entering. He became a close friend and, like his brother George, was a political pragmatist rather than a zealot on race at that time.

After Patterson won the governor's race, Gerald graduated. Gerald joined his brother George in the practice of law in Montgomery. He asked me to come practice with them. I decided not to do so, but Gerald remained a friend of the Ellzeys and mine, and, I think, was helpful to them in getting state contracts for sand and gravel in road-building projects.

Gerald, called "Sag" in law school, told me I was making a big mistake when I moved to Birmingham and volunteered to work in the campaign of Tom King, who had returned to Birmingham after serving as administrative assistant to the local congressman, George Huddleston. He had been persuaded to leave Washington and return to Birmingham and run for mayor. The form of government had recently been changed from the Commission form to Mayor-Council form.

Bull Connor Resists Integration

Bull Connor was police commissioner then. He had garnered national attention for resisting integration. Black people marched in the streets in protest of racial segregation. They boycotted stores and other businesses. Bull Connor's extreme actions while police commissioner led to a change in the form of city government. A group of young liberal lawyers and businessmen persuaded Tom to come home and run for mayor.

The race for mayor was going on when I arrived in Birmingham. I volunteered to work in Tom King's campaign office. After Tom lost to Art Hanes, he joined Chuck Morgan and Jim Shores in their fledgling law practice. Race was the determining factor in the election for mayor of Birmingham, too.

A Handshake Seals Tom King's Fate

Tom King lost to Art Hanes in the run-off election after the Hanes campaign alerted the *Birmingham News* to have a photographer at city hall. As Tom emerged, a black man offered his hand, and Tom shook it. The picture of him shaking hands with a black man on the steps of city hall was on the front page of the paper the next day — and the race was over.

But back to Selma when I left: A group of leaders got together and discussed forming a White Citizens Council. A group from Mississippi came to discuss how they had done it. In Mississippi there had been something called the Sovereignty Commission, that I think was created by the legislature. White Citizens Councils were created by people meeting for the purpose of formulating a plan to resist integration.

Almost all of the leaders in the community supported the forming of a White Citizens Council in Selma. Its ultimate aim was to resist integration, and it also was committed to preventing black people from registering to vote.

Dallas County's sheriff was a man named Jim Clark. He came to national attention for his role in preventing black people from registering to vote and later for preventing marchers seeking the right to vote from crossing the Edmund Pettus Bridge over the Alabama River on the march from Selma to Montgomery.

Clark was a personable man, on the surface very quiet and seemingly gentle. He was a close friend of the Ellzeys and we saw him regularly on a social basis. I think he was highly regarded by most of the leadership in Selma. There were frequent meetings and lots of discussion about what could be done about the trouble sure to come.

Montgomery Bus Boycott

Around this time, the Montgomery bus boycott got underway, and Montgomery was only 50 miles east of Selma. The local newspaper covered the story daily, and everybody also read the *Montgomery Advertiser*; and Montgomery TV stations were the source of television news in Selma.

Everybody was talking about the trouble in Montgomery and anticipating how it would soon come to Selma. The trouble in Montgomery referred to the boycott of the bus system by black people who refused to ride them after Rosa Parks refused to move to a seat in back of the bus.

There was also a lot of talk about a young black preacher who had come to the Dexter Avenue Methodist Church just down the street from the state capitol. People said that this Reverend Martin Luther King, Jr. was making trouble, stirring the black people up, suggesting a boycott of the buses, and preaching nonviolent resistance in his sermons.

There were lots of meetings and discussions about what should be done. These went on for a long time. I had already gotten into a little trouble with my father-in-law because I openly supported Kennedy in the 1960 presidential race. I had gotten some Kennedy literature from Birmingham and, with another woman, set up a stand opposite the courthouse and handed out Kennedy-for-President literature. Mr. Ellzey expressed some displeasure about it but did not insist that we stop.

I don't remember any of the local leaders being for John Kennedy but, as Election Day neared, one of Mr. Ellzey's close associates, Earl Goodwin, a state senator, called me and said I might be on the winning side after all. Interestingly, Kennedy did earn some of Alabama's electoral votes, but not all.

Jim Clark was the public figure at the head of the resistance to integration, but he was doing what the leadership wanted him to do. He was photographed keeping black people from entering the courthouse to register to vote and, of course, he got famous for being photographed with his deputies as they forcefully drove back the black protestors on their first effort to march across the Edmund Pettus Bridge.

The black people were driven back on their first try but came back later, better organized, and this time they were joined by notable people from all over the country, some then famous, others later to become famous. This second time the protestors succeeded and marched the entire 50 miles from Selma to Montgomery. This was made possible because Frank Johnson, the Federal District Judge for the Middle District in Montgomery, ordered Governor George Wallace to provide the marchers with police protection.

Even from this distance with the passage of time, it is difficult to understand how many good people could be oblivious to the concerns of the black people.

The Ellzeys, like their friends, seemed to truly love their domestic workers. They treated them kindly and paid them what was at that time the norm. They regularly inquired about their children, and helped them out financially and otherwise. If one of them got in trouble, they would do what was necessary to help them, but they were unyielding in their opposition to "mixing" with them.

Most of all, they were not going to allow the children to go to school with blacks. And they were unwilling to let blacks register to vote.

The first standoff between Sheriff Jim Clark and the black community was about that issue. When blacks showed up at the courthouse to register to vote, they were turned back forcibly by the sheriff and his people. He knew that he had the full support of the leaders of the community in doing so.

I certainly think he took his directions from the leaders of the community. The community leaders were meeting often, and many of these meetings took place at the Ellzey home. I was never asked to participate. The subject of the meetings was known to everyone. It became clear that preparations were being discussed about how to deal with the situation.

The discussion and organizing started while I was still in law school, and continued after I was out of law school and was clerking for Justice Simpson on the Alabama Supreme Court. At that time, I was still commuting.

I went to Montgomery every week or so, and they were organizing the local White Citizens Council and were explaining that this wouldn't affect Emma, their maid. Not any of our people, they said, would be adversely affected. They'll be allowed to attend whatever they wanted to attend. All they have to do is tell us in advance, and we'd make it all right for them to go.

People against the status quo had to have some kind of a pass to meet. They tried to stop the black people from meeting and planning mischief, I guess. They were enrolling people into the White Citizens Council, by name.

What I made clear concerning me is that I just simply refused to be a member of it, and it got heated, and that was a big source of consternation for several months. We just wouldn't mention it, but you know you can't talk without mentioning what's going on all around you.

By this time the situation had really gotten bad. I had graduated from law school. I was clerking for Judge Simpson in Montgomery, going back and forth again. One weekend we had another discussion about how I needed to join in, that I just needed to be a part of the family. And I said no, I'm sorry, I just cannot do it.

I shall not forget, Mr. Ellzey, whom I liked a lot, rather sadly said, "Then you are no longer a part of the family if you don't take part in this." It was painful for him to say it, I could tell. But that was the end of my life with them. I left the next day.

The Philadelphia Drexels

I had an office in Selma – not much of a practice, but I was earning enough to pay the rent and pay a secretary. Of course, as the newest lawyer in town, one got all the collection work one would handle. You got divorce cases and cases involving young people in trouble for minor misdemeanors.

I did get one significant client, and a significant piece of business involving the administration of a guardianship estate for one of the Drexel grandchildren, Anthony J. Drexel, III, of Pennsylvania.

The mother, who had custody of the minor children, moved to Selma and had to file accountings for the guardianship estate of the children until they reached majority. She was referred to me by one of the local Jewish merchants, of whom there were several prominent ones in Selma. That was the most significant piece of business I had.

The Drexel estate was being administered in Philadelphia, but this adjunct administration was going on in probate court in Dallas County, Selma. So, interestingly enough, she came to me because I was the only woman lawyer in town.

As the newest lawyer in town, I would get appointed to represent indigent criminal defendants where the law required that they have counsel.

Cecil Jackson, a law school classmate who was a year or so ahead of me, and I got appointed to represent a young black man accused of murder. I'd been out of law school about a year. Cecil was just a little before me. We worked on it like it was the most important case in the world, and, of course, it was to the client. And we did all right by him.

The jury convicted him of something less than capital murder, and he did not get the maximum sentence, but I got the distinct impression that we took the case a lot more seriously than the prosecution did. The defendant was a young black man, and the victim was a young black man, and the shooting occurred over a dispute during a poker game in which all of the players were black. I point this out to show that there were no racial overtones affecting the criminal prosecution of our defendant. Of course, the judge, the prosecutor, the jurors, and the lawyers for the defendant, Cecil and I, were all white.

Janie Joins the Bar

People often asked me how I was treated by the Selma Bar when I first started practicing there in 1959. I was invited to join the Bar Association when I first opened my office. Then that same lawyer who invited me came back a few days later and said, "Well, you can't come at this time because we have learned that the by-laws say that membership is limited to white males. We have to meet to amend the by-laws so that women can join." They accomplished that by eliminating the "male" part in the text, but not the "white" part. Membership remained limited to white lawyers for some years after that.

Arden: How were you treated regarding sex discrimination in law school?

Janie: Very little of that kind of discrimination. There were very few women there, of course, a total of five in different stages while I was there those three years, none in my class. Although the students were mostly all male, it was almost as though we shared a common enemy. We were all in this struggle to make it through the demanding curriculum together. There was not any overt discrimination by the students.

Arden: How about by the professors?

Janie: Well, every once in a while. I remember one of the professors asked my friend what she was doing in the library when he ran into her, and she said, "Looking up the outside case you told us to read." He said, "No, I mean, what are you doing in this law school? You know there are lots of men you may have kept out of a position."

This was not true, actually. When we went to law school, it was in the mid 50s. The World War II group had come and gone; therefore, the law school classes were really quite small. They got much, much bigger in the next decade. We weren't depriving any man of a seat at the table. And it was a long time before the student influx came back to the law school. Most men were pursuing other professions. Most everybody wanted to be an engineer in those years.

Alabama's First Female Law Professor

Arthur Weeks said (and I looked it up), "You won't be the first female law professor in America, but I believe you will be the first one on the east side of the Mississippi River." He used to make that public statement all the time later on when he'd introduce me.

I don't know whether it was true or not. I assumed there were one or two at Berkeley or somewhere. However, I was the first one in Alabama; I know that. When University of Alabama got a female professor, I had long been on the teaching staff at Cumberland.

Arden: What did you teach?

Janie: We didn't have many teachers, and therefore, you had more choices than you would have had if it had been more established. I taught a lot of things early on, but then I settled down to certain specialties.

I taught a lot of Procedure because I knew that topic better than anybody from my four years experience writing pleadings in the Mobile at-length common law pleadings. I also taught

Future Interests, Constitutional Law, Conflict of Laws (which I wound up teaching on a permanent basis), and a lot of things in the interim. I became the Advisor to the Law Review when we started one and I ran the clinical program for a while.

Arden: When did you get divorced?

Janie: Well, we weren't in a hurry about it. We didn't fall out with each other. Bless his heart, it never dawned on Bill to cross his daddy on anything. In particular not on something major like his wife refusing to join the White Citizens Council.

Anyway, I went to Birmingham and had the usual excuses from law firms. They claimed that they had no objection to hiring a woman lawyer, but the clients would never accept it.

Coincidentally, the Dean of the University Law School, Leigh Harrison, a very quiet, unassuming man, and one of the best teachers I ever had, whom I adored, recommended me to Liberty National Life Insurance Company, located in Birmingham.

I had a special poignancy about Dean Harrison because of an incident that occurred in our senior year. He was a very private, shy man, quite remote. I never had a personal conversation with him. But I knew from his calling on me in class as another student was presenting a case that he knew I worked hard and tried to understand what he was trying to convey in class.

In any event, I was in the rotunda reading the notices to students that were routinely posted there. One day, I was reading a notice that law firms would be visiting the school at a specific time and were interested in interviewing students. Some firm notices restricted the invitation to be interviewed to those students with grade points over some specified point, i.e., 2.0 or higher.

All Qualified and Nowhere to Work

Dean Harrison saw me reading these notices and came up to me with obvious embarrassment, or at least obvious discomfort, and remarked, "You know you are not included in this." It was obviously painful for him to tell me this. I knew that the reason he had done so was to save me the pain and embarrassment of being told that at an attempted interview. It was an embarrassing moment for both of us and never produced any long discussion. I just responded, "I know" and moved on. But I have never forgotten the effort he made to save me from even more pain.

I never knew how a recommendation from Dean Harrison led to an interview with Liberty National, but I have always suspected that it had something to do with that moment in the Rotunda. Of course, there were bound to have been connections between the officers and directors of Liberty National and the law school. I never inquired, but the offer came shortly after an experience I had with the then-President of the Alabama Bar Association.

Dean Harrison had suggested that I ask his advice. I called for an appointment and explained that Dean Harrison had suggested that I ask his advice about the best way to go about getting a job with a law firm in Birmingham. He, the then-president of the bar, was a partner in the biggest and oldest firm in Birmingham.

He was courteous and seemingly sympathetic but repeated the same story I had encountered at other firms: that the lawyers in the firm would have no problem with a female lawyer; in fact, he said, his firm had one of long standing who worked with the partner who handled the firm's bond business; but, he emphasized, she did not deal directly with clients.

He shared the opinion that others had expressed: the firms' clients would not feel comfortable with a female lawyer. He suggested that I consider trying to get a job with the house counsel for one of the corporations in town. I knew that his firm represented most, if not all of them, and asked him to suggest one or more. He mentioned the insurance companies in town, Liberty National and Protective Life.

He also mentioned Vulcan Materials, a local company that mined and processed gravel, etc., for road construction, I assumed from my in-laws' business. He did not offer to call or otherwise introduce me.

I decided to call on Vulcan Materials' corporate office that was located in Mountain Brook. I somehow knew that its CEO Barney Monaghan was a prominent Catholic. I don't know exactly how I knew that, but somehow I must have heard or seen something about him at Vincent Kilborn's office that, as I might have mentioned, represented the Catholic Diocese of Mobile, which included Birmingham.

I presented myself at Vulcan Materials' offices and asked to speak to Mr. Monaghan. I was told he was out of town, and a young male lawyer in the office asked the nature of my business.

He expressed utter disbelief when I told him why I was there. He said that he simply could not imagine that Mr. Arant had suggested that Vulcan might consider a woman lawyer.

He went on to explain that although it was the corporate office, laborers, truck drivers, and other support personnel were often about, implying that a woman had no business in such an environment. I left without an interview.

The thought of concentrating the search on corporate legal offices persisted, and in a few days I did get an appointment with Ira Burleson, general counsel for Liberty National Life Insurance Company. With the concurrence of Mr. Ehney

Camp, Vice President in charge of the investment division of the company, Burleson gave me a job as legal adviser to the Investment Division, which suited me.

It was a pleasant experience, and I learned a lot. I had always had an interest in the financial markets and wanted to know more about the world of finance.

I stayed there until Laura was born.

Arden: How did you meet Laura's dad, Jim Shores?

Janie: One of my friends from law school is named John David Snodgrass. He was in love with my friend, Annette. They entered law school when I was a senior, and she and I became good friends. Annette Clark, from Sheffield, and John David, from Scottsboro, were a year or so behind me in law school. I became very fond of both of them, and through them I met Jim.

John David had a car wreck in Birmingham two or three years earlier while he was in undergraduate school, at Five Points South, it's one of the main intersections. It happened late at night; he claimed it wasn't his fault, but he ran into a carload of black kids. He said it looked as though there were fourteen of them who jumped out and ran in every direction.

Enter Jim Shores

The police came, and John David called his dad, a circuit judge in Scottsboro, and asked him which lawyers he should get to represent him. He recommended two lawyers who were then practicing together in Birmingham, Chuck Morgan and Jim Shores.

Jim and Chuck were in Tuscaloosa and, I think, called John David to meet for a drink; he called Annette to join them, and she asked me to come along. It was not unusual for the three of us to find someplace cool on those August afternoons.

I was in effect finished with law school and was just waiting for school to end in August 1959. Annette and John David were in summer school.

It was unbearably hot in Tuscaloosa that year, and we developed a pattern of going to the movies or somewhere every afternoon just to get out of the hot apartment. Annette and I shared an apartment that summer. My car was air-conditioned; I don't think John David's was. So we took road trips, often to Birmingham to visit anywhere it was cool.

Arden: Tell me about your class notes. You said you shared them with friends. Did you copyright them?

Janie: I didn't think of that then. I just shared them with anybody who wanted them. I didn't think about, you know, copyrights. I made what I called a summary of the cases and class notes. It was my way of reducing the masses of material to something manageable.

We were required to read a designated number of cases each day. The so-called case method was used in all law schools. I summarized my class notes and cases into one study document that I called a "summary." I shared those summaries with friends, and somewhere in the process the notes were reproduced and later sold. I didn't learn about this until much later. *Janie's Summaries* eventually were being sold at the local bookstore.

I'd been gone for years and I called the book store and asked whether it was true that my summaries were being sold.. "Come on," I said, "are you selling those summaries?" I don't even know if they remained the notes that I originally had written because the document had been through so many hands. No telling what it said after several years. "You sell them with my name on them?" He said he couldn't sell them without that.

No telling how many years folks continued to do that. I run into people even today who say, "I would have never gotten out of Future Interests, or some other class without *Janie's Summaries*."

That gave me some notoriety in the legal community, and I'm sure that those who used *Janie's Summaries*, if it helped them, couldn't help but be for me. I learned that this familiarity was a broader exposure to the legal community over the state than most practicing lawyers would ever have.

Law School Days

Arden: Tell me something about some of your classmates.

Janie: I was especially close to a classmate named Charles McPherson Augustin Rogers, III or, as we called him, Max. I entered law school at mid-year. I did not take any classes that summer so that I could get back with my group. You see, I was a semester ahead of them. I was trying to get back with the ones I was supposed to be with.

I took off and didn't take much, no more than three or four hours. So when I came back in the fall, there was the new fall class, which I was in. We all took the exams at the end of the fall semester, and Max Rogers just about matched me in terms of high grades.

There had never been anybody close to my grades level before. Being tied in terms of class standing brings you together; for example, if you're moot court partners, or you're on law review, or competing for editor-in-chief and such. Max and I became very good friends. He was from an old Mobile family. His father was in an old Mobile law firm. Max came back to Mobile and practiced there, until much later, when he became president of one of the local banks in Mobile. He and I had a wonderful relationship.

Annette started law school that fall, and I was in classes with her. That's how I got to know John David. He wasn't in law school yet.

It was through the law school activities that I got to have a social network in that way. After I made such good grades the first year and shared my summaries, I held informal seminars to prepare for the exams and got more and more students every time. There are no mid-term exams in law school; everything depends on finals. You can imagine if you hadn't paid attention in class the whole year, and not made good study notes, what a massive undertaking it would be to get ready for the all-important final exam. I did not mind helping other people prepare for the finals because doing so helped me prepare. Due to this, I never had an enemy in law school.

I had a professor once who wrote on my exam, "You must have had a friend who's had this course earlier." I went to see him and asked him "What does that mean?" He said, "Well, it's almost word for word what I said." And it was! You know, I told him why. It insulted me that he would assume that I must have cheated somehow or other and that I got the answers from somewhere else. But, you know, I'd quoted him word for word, and it's hard for anybody to disagree with his own words.

Al Ritchey was another close friend. He's from Birmingham from a Lebanese family. One of my Mobile friends mentioned from time to time that Al was Lebanese, as though that was something I should know. Mobile can be a somewhat snobbish town, and my Mobile friends would remark, "You know, we just don't pal around with the Greeks and the Lebanese."

Well, that made no sense at all to me. Baldwin County was made up of varieties of ethnic communities. Italians settled in Daphne. Greeks founded the town of Malbis. Germans settled in Foley. I had been surrounded by people of different ethnicities all my life so I didn't know that mingling supposedly was forbidden until I went to law school. It was just one of those irrational prejudices.

Arden: Who else influenced you from law school?

Janie: People senior to me. We had a professor, I think he was the assistant dean, too, who was a nice person, but he must have hated confrontation.

Some professors respond immediately and aggressively when they call on you to give a case, and you have to say you're not prepared. The usual response is to just jump on them, and others, like this one, I don't think he knew how to do that. He was uncomfortable doing it. He didn't want to hear, "I'm not prepared, sir."

I was the only woman in the class, and the class was small, so rather than risk his discomfort, he just called on me for all of the cases. My male classmates knew that he was doing that to avoid confronting them. They would make a joke of it, saying things like, "Janie, you got all the cases ready today?" I felt sad for that professor. He called on me repeatedly to recite a case so that he wouldn't have to deal with an "unprepared" answer. The students became my friends because they knew I knew what they were doing. Most of that bunch became good lawyers. Almost all joined established firms. I didn't blame them as much as I did the professor. He let them control the class instead of controlling it himself.

Cakes & Cookbooks by Morris & Millard

Arden: Who was it that founded the Southern Poverty Law Center?

Janie: Morris Dees. He was in law school at the same time I was, as was the Habitat for Humanity founder, Millard Fuller.

Morris Dees and Millard Fuller were a team. Both of them came from poor families and they thought up clever ways to make ends meet.

People said that Morris used to plow up the dirt roads near where his family lived so he could make money by pulling people out when they got stuck in the rough mud. He had the tractor there waiting, and he'd pull them out and charge them five dollars. He could figure out how to make money, and he did.

I like the story about the birthday cakes. When students signed up for classes in those days, there were no computers. Sign-up would be done by signing for classes on paper lists laid out at long tables in the basketball stadium. If you wanted to take English 101, you'd get in line to sign up at the table marked for that course.

You might spend all day, filling out your name and address, and so on, for every course. Well, at the end of the line, Morris just set up another table where he'd also take your name and address, birthday, your parents' address. Then to everyone who signed with a parent's address, he'd send a letter saying that for ten dollars he would guarantee delivery of a personalized birthday cake to their son or daughter while they were a freshman at the University of Alabama. Well, you know a lot of folks would pay to get that delivered.

He took the orders to the local bakery and cut a deal. They'd bake them and deliver them, and Morris kept the difference. He's just that clever. Millard and he were partners in that cake endeavor. I'm not certain whether or not Morris headed it up; I bet he did.

They also had a business selling fresh laurel wreaths at Christmas time. Then Morris branched out into cookbooks. Got all the members of the faculty at the University of Alabama to write their favorite recipes, then put those into a cookbook; it was all faculty recipes as well as famous people's. Rumor had it that Jackie Kennedy sent in a recipe, of all things.

Morris is an entrepreneur; his mind works that way; and Millard, they say, he went into business with him. For years, Morris and he had an impressive law practice championing civil rights. Millard told him that when he'd made a million dollars, he was going to quit. Millard wanted to be a missionary, and he planned do it when he made a million dollars.

Well, he did exactly that. Millard moved on to establish Habitat for Humanity, in Americus, Georgia. Isn't that wonderful? And Morris went on to run the Southern Poverty Law Center in Montgomery, which is a very big, important operation now doing crucial human rights work.

My classmates were a colorful, impressive bunch, and diverse.

George Wallace's brother, Sag, was another good friend. Sag was older than the rest of us. He'd been to law school and then had to go off to war, and he got tuberculosis, I think, and lost a lung.

I never shall forget when Sputnik, the first artificial Earth satellite went up; remember that? You might have been too young. Sputnik 1 went up in 1957. It was a big thing that the Russians had accomplished. I remember a bunch of really mean boys in law school took a picture of Sag, George Wallace's brother, with his scar where he'd lost his lung. It's a big scar. And Cecil Jackson, Sag's good friend, had polio as a child, and his legs were all shriveled up. They took pictures of them and tried to post them to the Russians as our astronauts. I'm not sure what message they thought they were sending.

"Out-Segged"

George Wallace ran for governor the first time in 1958 while we were all in law school. All of us had a candidate – mine was Jimmy Faulkner, James H. Faulkner from Bay Minette, Alabama, who was the publisher of the *Baldwin Press*, the local Baldwin County newspaper. He was from Baldwin County; that was why I was for him.

The liberal in the bunch was George Hawkins from Gadsden. He'd been in the Senate. He had the support of the labor unions.

Another candidate for governor, John Patterson, was famous because his daddy had been shot and killed while running for Attorney General. He was from Phenix City, Alabama, a place notorious for gambling. The county was controlled by gambling interests, and they were concerned he was going to shut down the gambling enterprises if he was elected Attorney General.

John Patterson had that notoriety going for him in the race for governor in 1958. The case of *Brown v. Board of Education* was decided in 1954, so by the '58 governor's race there was but one issue, and that was race. John Patterson was the one who seized on that by being pro-segregation, and he beat George Wallace in a run-off. After that, Wallace said that he'd never be "out-segged" again. Formerly, Wallace had been kind of the moderate on that issue. George Hawkins was the liberal. That switch really had an impact on the state of Alabama from then on.

Arden: In what way?

Janie: Race became the only issue in the 1958 governor's campaign; it dominated Alabama politics for the next forty years and still does. The problems just kept getting worse during the '60s and the Civil Rights movement, and the assassinations of leaders, and so on. Lyndon Johnson was right when he said that the South was lost to the Democrats from the moment President Johnson signed the Civil Rights Act that Congress finally passed after John Kennedy was killed.

It's interesting to think what might have been the outcome if we had just had some leadership in Alabama to say we have to deal with this; but nobody in power in the South did. Georgia was just as backward. Arkansas was just as bad. Louisiana was just as bad.

I don't remember much about Florida, but it's not a true Southern state anyway. There are so many people who settle there who are not from the South.

Race played a part in my own political campaign when I qualified to run for a vacancy on the Alabama Supreme Court in 1972. By that time, I'd been on the faculty of Cumberland for eight or nine years. So I had that many classes of lawyers whom I taught there who knew me. Of course, my law school classmates from the 1950s knew who I was, and as it turned out, a lot more lawyers knew who I was because they had benefitted from those course summaries I wrote that had been passed down.

Judge Simpson's Law Clerk

Also helping my public recognition was my association with Judge Simpson. When I first got out of law school, I was hired as Judge Simpson's law clerk on the Supreme Court because Vince Kilborn recommended me. Judge Simpson was a delightful man and a completely fair judge. Not once in our long association did I see any bias in favor of one side over the other. My charge was to apply the law without regard to the outcome.

Many of the judges were elderly back then. Because there was no retirement program for judges in Alabama, most of them continued to serve well beyond standard retirement age. That problem was not fixed until Howell Heflin came along much later. Heflin managed to get a retirement system for judges enacted by the legislature. Before that happened, few judges ever retired; they just continued to stay on the bench until they died and the then-governor appointed somebody else. It became increasingly difficult as they got older for them to handle the demanding work load of the court.

I clerked for Judge Simpson after I graduated from law school. I went back and forth to Montgomery from Selma. He was used to the fact that I was not physically there all the time, and that worked out fine. I'd go and get two or three case files at a time, work on them and bring them back and get some more. I worked for him that first year, then I came back and opened my office in Selma. Then the race issues in Selma all blew up, and I moved to Birmingham.

Shortly after I got to Birmingham, Judge Simpson was in a bad car wreck, and his secretary called me and said, "The judge just can't function as well as he once did," and asked if I would help him out while he was recovering. And I did. He was physically impaired, but his mind was as sharp as it had always been. There was no doubt that his legal opinions were his opinions. The other judges knew that he was mentally alert and capable of making decisions. I continued to help him for quite a long time, even while I was teaching at Cumberland Law School.

Laura is Born

Arden: How did being a woman during that time influence what happened to you?

Janie: After law school, and after I moved to Birmingham and married Jim Shores, my daughter Laura was born in 1964. I was on the faculty at Cumberland, and actually, I felt that I didn't belong in either world then. I wasn't available for carpooling and the various motherly activities as much as I should have been. In addition, I was out there in the law school in a man's world, in a sense.

I didn't feel that I belonged anywhere. I felt there was a lot of resentment from the women, the other mothers of Laura's little friends, toward me. I never quite understood it.

It seemed to me they were saying, "Well, you're not doing your part in that traditional role." I don't know how to explain it, but I felt I was "damned if you do and damned if you don't."

When Jim Shores and I married, he was practicing law with Chuck Morgan. Tom King had been beaten in the race for mayor of Birmingham. That battle was determined by race. Art Hanes had the support of the KKK, and Tom was depicted as being too soft on the only issue that seemed to matter.

I had not avoided racial strife by leaving Selma. Racial tensions also were rampant in Birmingham. Black people boycotted department stores; their houses were bombed during the night; children marched in the streets. The Freedom Riders were coming through on buses. Bull Connor served as Birmingham's Commissioner of Public Safety in the '60s. His ideologies focused his official orders in direct opposition to the Civil Rights Movement. Connor turned fire hoses and police dogs on children and protesters in the parks.

Jim Shores and Chuck Morgan were often seen as representing the "wrong" side from the standpoint of social acceptance in Alabama. Tom King had been persuaded to move home and run for mayor right in the middle of all the race problems. Remember, he was defeated when he was walking out of city hall and shook hands with a black man going up the steps, and the *Birmingham News* captured that picture and ran it the next morning in the paper. That was the end of Tom King's campaign. He joined Jim and Chuck's law practice.

Chuck Morgan Speaks Out

Racial tension was palpable then and it got worse. One Sunday morning in the fall of 1963 a bomb exploded in the 16th Street Baptist Church and four young black girls were killed. The city was stunned, but it was not the first time bombs had been involved. This time seemed worse somehow.

Then, after the bombing, Chuck spoke to the Young Men's Businessmen's Club and said, "We're to blame, you and I as citizens; we are to blame for what's happening. You businessmen are to blame." He wasn't quite run out of town, but he just about was. Not long after that, Chuck decided to move to Atlanta. Later, Harper & Row published his fine book about those times called *A Time To Speak*.

Chuck was gone, and Jim was left with the office. And Birmingham was left with sorrow, anger, and unsolved tensions. I heard the bomb blast from my house on Red Mountain that day. It was September 12, 1963.

We knew many of the prominent black leaders in town. Dr. A. G. Gaston was the local black millionaire. Arthur Shores was a prominent black lawyer, one of the first black lawyers admitted to the bar in Alabama. His house was bombed with regularity during those years, so everybody knew who this Lawyer Shores was. Arthur Shores' home phone was unlisted, but Jim Shores' phone was listed; so Jim got calls from everybody looking for Arthur Shores.

Some of these calls for Arthur were from out of state media. Jim passed along to Arthur any that appeared to be legitimate but did not disclose Arthur's home number.

We were out of favor socially in Birmingham because of the kinds of cases Jim and Chuck handled. Chuck relished the civil rights work more than Jim did, but Jim did his fair share of the unpopular ones and was as committed as Chuck to doing all that he could.

It is hard to overstate the effect that the Supreme Court's decision in *Brown v. the Board of Education* had in the South and in Alabama in particular. For example, Hugo Black, a native son of Alabama who had represented Alabama in the U.S. Senate before being appointed to the United States Supreme Court by President Roosevelt, was reviled in Alabama for his supporting vote in that case. The local legislature passed resolutions declaring the decision "null and void" in Alabama. Alabama's Secretary of State was quoted as saying of Judge Black, "I hope he dies and burns in hell." Black was not invited to his law school 50th reunion in 1956. Alabama was mad!

Another casualty of the racial storm sweeping the state was Paul Johnston. Paul and his brother Joseph were partners in their father's law firm, one of the oldest and most prestigious in Birmingham. Paul was considered a liberal by local social and business standards. He was a member of the Lawyers Committee for Civil Rights Under Law, which "proved" he was. In any event, Paul got caught up in the civil rights debate and rumor had it that he was asked to leave the family firm.

One Gary Thomas Rowe had been arrested in connection with the murder of Viola Liuzzo, a white woman from "up North" who joined the voting rights march from Selma to Montgomery. Paul got a call from a friend in the Kennedy administration asking him to help Rowe, who was really working undercover for the FBI. I think the friend who called Paul was Nick Katzenbach, a classmate from Yale Law School then serving as deputy attorney general.

Paul's family firm decided they could not be connected to such an "unsavory" matter as civil rights, so Paul was asked to leave. I think Chuck Morgan had left Jim's Birmingham practice to move to Atlanta by this time. Paul came to Jim and asked if he could join the practice, such as it was.

When I ran for the Supreme Court in 1972, I thought that race would be an issue, but not the defining one. It wasn't a crucial issue but it did play a part. My most serious opposition was Eric Embry. Eric was a good lawyer with the prestigious Birmingham Beddow Law Firm. Eric had represented *The New York Times* before the Supreme Court of the United States, *New York Times v. Sullivan*, a landmark decision holding that a person gives up some of their privacy when they hold public office. Sullivan had been the police commissioner in Montgomery. Last to qualify as a candidate was a little known lawyer who ran under the name Jimmy Faulkner.

The Case of the Two Jimmys

Most of the candidates didn't amount to very much politically. But James H. Faulkner ran, not the other Jimmy Faulkner from Baldwin County. I had to call around and find out who this other Jimmy was. Nobody in town knew. He was a sole practitioner out in Shelby County somewhere, and his friends told him he ought to run because he would have the benefit of the same name as the well-known Jimmy Faulkner who had run for governor.

Campaign workers told the faux Jimmy Faulkner that with two Faulkners running, he might get votes from hoodwinked fans of the well-regarded "real" Jimmy Faulkner. As it turned out, that was clever reasoning. The run-off came down to the faux Faulkner and me. Faulkner and his supporters told voters that I was the black Arthur Shores' wife. The names were so well known, the Faulkner name and the Shores name, that it just made all his lies work perfectly.

We didn't have much money to spend in the run-off. I didn't have much to spend in the entire campaign. My supporters were worried that we might lose because the voters were thinking that I was black and that the Jimmy on the ballot was the well-regarded Jimmy Faulkner.

My supporters were calling from all over the state to say that we needed to do something to convince the voters of their mistakes. I agreed that the effort to confuse the voters was working, but it was a difficult assignment. What could we do? He wasn't who he claimed he was, and I was not who he claimed I was, but we couldn't change our names.

No doubt that trick was the reason for the outcome of that race. I lost.

However, in two years' time, I ran again and won.

Interview II

A Dog Named Democrat

Remembrance of Friends Past

Arden: Who were some of the people from that early period of time who influenced the choices that you made?

Janie: The only other employee in the Kilborn office when I started working there was Frances Hart, and she was funny, not married. During World War II, she had served in the WAVES, the female branch of the Navy. She served quite a number of years. She believed that women were just as good at any assignment as men were. She did not believe that being female constituted a handicap no matter what it was you were interested in doing. That was refreshing to me to have my own notions confirmed.

Frances taught me how to smoke. After I had been there a while, I got up the nerve to mention her smoking. I told her that it didn't bother me at work but the smoke got in my hair, and I had to shampoo it every night before I could go to sleep. She said "Honey, it wouldn't bother you at all if you smoked, too." So, I practiced and soon was smoking, too. Frances was right, I was no longer bothered by the smoke. I smoked until Laura was about six years old.

Of the friends I had in high school, most got married right away to their high school sweethearts. One or two also went to Mobile and got jobs in offices. But most of them just got married right away and most of them worked. You know, they were very successful marriages, very successful lives, as far as

I've been able to tell. Seem to be very happy, almost never moving out of Baldwin County.

Arden: Do you think the fact that many of your peers were marrying right out of high school also influenced your decision to marry young?

Janie: Maybe, but mostly I saw that as a means of helping my going to school. I don't think I was crass enough to think I could wrangle up a college degree out of the association, and I always continued to work; but marriage made the process easier, there's just no question about it. I'm forever grateful for that boost to my efforts. We didn't have lots of money, but Bill Ellzey worked for his father. We didn't have to worry about the basics, as I certainly would have had to do if I were totally on my own.

I don't think his parents ever forgave me for having pursued my career. I think they would have loved for us to have had children, for me to be a "proper" daughter-in-law who stayed home and looked after children. Well, I just wasn't. But I had absolutely no intention at all to hurt Bill, and I was saddened that we parted on such an awful note.

Integration troubles certainly had begun before I left, but shortly after I moved, Selma made national news and became a symbol of racial intolerance in the South. Selma was depicted as being brutal and intolerant. Pictures on national television did little to persuade the rest of the world that Selma was a nice place to live, for white or black people. It was awful. That same Sheriff Jim Clark who had prevented black people from registering to vote was now preventing them by brute force from crossing the Edmond Pettus Bridge.

Through me, the Ellzeys met my friend Sag Wallace, George Wallace's brother. Sag and Mrs. Ellzey became fishing buddies, and that friendship was good for Mr. Ellzey's business. The senior Ellzey was in the sand, gravel, and concrete business, and sand and gravel are necessary components in highway building. I'm sure that connection to the Wallace administration was fruitful for him during the Wallace years, which lasted interminably. But we never discussed it. I never saw the senior Ellzeys again after I left there.

Bill, bless his heart, would phone me every once in a while. He promptly found a new girlfriend. I had seen her. She was a very pretty woman. She was on the local television as the weather girl. You remember when they used to have pretty women give the weather at the beginning of the TV?

Arden: Still do.

Janie: She was a lovely looking woman. He called me in Birmingham once to tell me she was having some kind of psychological problems and was in a hospital in Birmingham; he wanted to know if I thought it would help her if I went to see her. I thought, "I'll be damned. What on earth causes you to think that would be of any comfort to her?" If I had thought there was anything I could have done, I would have. But there was nothing I could think of to improve her situation.

No, I never met her, but later, I'm told, she wrote a nice tribute to him that was published, at least locally. Bill was killed in an automobile accident within a very few years. They had two children together, two boys.

Bill's younger sister was much younger than he was. She was a teenager when I was part of the family. She married and went to live in Birmingham, where her husband was the principal of a local high school, I forget which one. Her name was Marie. She and I were close when I was in the family. I always was delighted to see her, and know that she was doing well.

Out of the Frying Pan

I left Selma in the early 1960s because of a violent disagreement over what our response to the Civil Rights movement was to be. When I got to Birmingham, the unrest was as bad or worse. We had the Freedom Riders, church bombings, Bull Connor and fire hoses, police dogs, beatings, all making national news. One Sunday, I remember exactly where I was when the bomb went off in the 16th Street Baptist Church, killing children inside.

Arden: What was it like dating your future husband during that period of time?

Janie: Well, it wasn't like dating, at all. I was busy all the time. We, along with most of our crowd, were trying to help Tom King get elected. He was also busy all the time practicing law, trying to keep the practice running as Tom and Chuck Morgan devoted themselves to the campaign. We just kind of met doing those things. After Tom lost the election, I got a job, finally. Jim Shores and I married in '62, I think.

When I moved to Birmingham, I bought myself a lot, paid down on it, and was trying to find somebody to build a house on it, on top of the mountain overlooking the city.

John and Willie, my parents, came to Birmingham to see me, probably en route to see one or both of John's sisters, who lived near Birmingham. They did that far more often than coming to spend the night with me. I showed John my lot. He looked at it and said, "Janie, you haven't bought a lot, you've bought a hole on top of this mountain."

I got reacquainted with Jim (we hadn't fallen completely, madly in love in the beginning) over that house. Jim had a client who was a builder of sorts, and was going to see what we could work out with respect to the house. It sits right over the city. I was in that house when I heard the bombs aimed at black churches and activists go off in Birmingham. The bombs that day in 1963 killed four black girls in the 16th Street Baptist Church. Terrible.

Laura was born in January 1964, at which point I would have been 31 or 32. By that time, I was working at Liberty National in the trust department.

Laura was a year or so old when the dean of the law school called me and offered me a job teaching; and that was a perfectly wonderful opportunity. While Laura was little, teaching gave me more flexibility than a nine-to-five job and that was very attractive to me. That worked really well; I had some time with her.

Bob and Helen Vance

At about the time I met Jim Shores, he already knew Bob and Helen Vance, and we all became close friends. They are godparents to Laura. She was very fond of them.

The Vances were both good Democrats and were active in party politics. For many years, Bob was chairman of the state Democratic Committee. They became our closest friends. We saw them often as our children grew up. In fact we had Chinese takeout usually at their house, every Sunday night. They had two sons, Robert and Charles. Robert was a year or so older than Laura and Charles was about a year younger. Laura remains close to Robert and his wife, Joyce. Incidentally, I performed their marriage ceremony, and it took. They have a wonderful family of their own now.

Of course, the children went off to college and law school and didn't see much of each other during those years.

Robert attended the University of Virginia Law School where he met Joyce, and Laura went to Smith for undergraduate school and to the University of Chicago Law

School. Laura had a wonderful year serving as Bob's law clerk when she finished law school.

Bob and I had competed for an appointment by Jimmy Carter to the then 5th, now 11th United States Court of Appeals. He was killed shortly after Laura's year with him. A package came in the mail to him at home and it contained a homemade bomb that blew up when he opened it in the kitchen. He was killed instantly, and Helen was badly injured. A disgruntled litigant was convicted, but we will never know all of the story.

I was very fond of Helen and Bob. Our relationship lasted a long time. I was in Birmingham to speak at their daughter-in-law's investiture as a United States Attorney in Birmingham. She was appointed by Barack Obama and is still serving. She is a smart girl from California. She and Robert have a lovely family, hopefully all good Democrats.

Robert is a Circuit Judge in Birmingham. He ran for Chief Justice but was beaten by Roy Moore. Moore was elected again after having been removed from office for refusing to obey a court order to remove the Ten Commandments monument that he had installed illegally in the Supreme Court building when he was Chief Justice — only in Alabama! Now he is in the news again for ordering Probate Judges not to perform same-sex marriages, in spite of the U.S. Supreme Court decision approving them.

Bob, Helen, Jim and I were continually active in Democratic politics. Bob was the chairman of the Democratic Executive Committee for many years. He and George Wallace were at odds frequently over issues of various kinds.

Wallace made an effort to seize control of the party at one point. Bob heard that he was seeking support from members of the executive committee before its annual meeting. The executive committee consisted of twenty-two people from around the state. Before the meeting, Bob made a motion that carried to increase the number of committee members from 22 to 72 or some such number therefore denying George Wallace's majority. Eventually, Bob and George Wallace got to be very friendly before they both died.

Dog Days

Helen has always raised dogs, always. The breeds varied from time to time. One time she was into Great Danes, another time it was English Sheepdogs. She always had dogs and they showed at Westminster. She didn't show them herself, but she worked with people to show her dogs. George Wallace sent Helen a fine dog, indicating, I guess, that 'all is now forgiven; now we can show our love for these dogs, at least.' I think it was a Great Dane. She named that dog Democrat.

Arden: What about James' and your relationship with George Wallace? How did you feel about him?

Janie: Well, Sag came to see me when he heard I was serious about Jim to warn me that Jim Shores and Chuck Morgan were so liberal that I would never amount to anything politically if I married into that group.

Arden: What did you say to that?

Janie: Well, I said, "Thank you, Sag," but I told Jim about it, and he was as mad as fire. He wasn't fond of George Wallace to start with. I don't think that we disliked him personally. We disagreed with him politically. But everybody liked Sag. Rumor has it that Sag was probably the bagman during the several Wallace administrations, but he was a likable person.

I think George Wallace was not an evil man. He was a politician to the bone. There is a book about George Wallace by an historian over at Emory University that is as accurate as any history book I've ever read and well done, too. It is called

The Politics of Rage by Dan T. Carter. Lots of work went into it. I think it captures the essence of Wallace better than any other work on the subject.

I always believed that Wallace was simply driven to gain political office, and he knew that the race issue would work to his benefit. I don't think deep down that he believed all of the outrageous things he did and said. He just knew what would move people. That doesn't make what he did any more honorable.

When I got to Birmingham, I re-met the old-line Democrats that I had known earlier, including Bob and Helen Vance and Jim Shores. We suffered through President Kennedy's assassination and the whole aftermath. It made a lasting bond among the people who were, in a way, "outsiders" down here even then.

As I mentioned earlier, in 1958 John Patterson beat Wallace for governor. Patterson supported Kennedy. I've always had a little soft spot for that, and delivered four or five '68 Democratic convention delegates to Kennedy from Alabama that he wouldn't have had otherwise. But Alabama didn't completely go for him.

Arden: Were you ever a delegate to a convention?

Janie: No, I never did run. Bob always was there, of course, he was there as chairman of the party, too. He was at the one that blew up, and the Dixiecrats bolted out; Strom Thurmond led the revolt, and George Wallace was with him. The Civil Rights Act and the Voting Rights Act occurred after Kennedy was killed, and this was the next convention after that.

The race issue severed the Democratic Party in the South and it's never made a recovery. George Wallace used campaign tactics to create negative images on topics people knew nothing about. Twisting the truth to suit your campaign goals has had long-term corrupting effects on U.S. politics.

Lyndon Johnson foresaw that when he signed the Voting Rights Act in 1965, the South would be lost to the Democratic Party for generations. Here we are fifty years later, and the South remains solidly Republican, almost surely because of the race issue. We're not over that struggle yet. It's discouraging to me today to look from that perspective and see it all repeating itself on the national scene now. We don't learn fast.

Arden: I know you were teaching law at Samford. What steered you toward running for the Supreme Court?

Heflin Fights for Constitutional Amendment

Janie: Well, I left out a section. My first year out of law school, I drove back and forth to Montgomery from Selma and clerked for Judge Simpson. And the judges were old. Up until 1972, there were no retirement benefits, so nobody ever retired.

Judge Simpson had an automobile accident that left him impaired somewhat. He called me and asked me if I could help him with his cases. As it turned out, I was happy to; it was wonderfully convenient to me. I was teaching out at the Cumberland law school and had easy access to the library, so writing opinions for Judge Simpson was entirely compatible. So I was pleased to be helping him and just continued to do so because he never did get much better.

In the meantime, my longtime friend and Jim's longtime friend, a good Democrat, ran for the Chief Justice position, the Chief Justice having finally died. I don't think he ever retired. But, anyhow, Howell Heflin was a sole practitioner in Tuscumbia, Alabama, a workhorse. He's one of those people who just works all the time. He ran for the position of Chief Justice and was elected in 1972. And he immediately went about absolutely devoting full time to getting a constitutional amendment rewriting the entire judicial article, revamping the court system entirely. It was a hodgepodge of courts of special jurisdiction.

As counties grew and circuit courts couldn't handle increasing caseloads, local judges and lawyers working with their legislators would come up with a local bill to create a special court to take care of some of the load. So we had God knows how many different kinds of those. And they established their own rules of procedure and practice, making it difficult for lawyers from other counties to conduct business there.

So Heflin set about rewriting the provisions of the constitution dealing with courts and establishing a modern, unified judicial system. After a lot of work and commitment, a new Judicial Article was drafted and put on the ballot for adoption by the voters. Of course, all of that work and effort would not amount to anything unless the people in a statewide referendum adopted it as a part of the constitution.

We worked like dogs to get it passed. I made speeches, mostly to women's groups around the state. The League of Women Voters was especially supportive, I recall, but other groups were also helpful. There was much debate about when we should put the subject to a vote. A statewide election was required and the question was: should we put the constitutional amendment on the ballot standing alone, or would it gain more support if it were included on the ballot in a general election, say for governor? I believed it had a better chance if it were on the ballot standing alone. Then only those voters with a specific interest were likely to vote. I suggested a special election to be held the day before Christmas as an ideal time. Another member of the working committee suggested the day of the Alabama/Auburn game.

This partial constitutional reform created a unified court system consisting of District Courts and Circuit Courts with uniform jurisdiction throughout the state, eliminating all of those inferior courts that had been created as local needs demanded. It also established a retirement system for judges, and it got Alabama on the map as being one of the most progressive states in the United States as far as the court system was concerned. It was a proud moment for all of us.

Arden: When was Heflin elected Chief Justice?

Janie: In 1970. When I ran in '72, he was not on the ballot. Howell had been Chief Justice for four years when I was elected after I ran again in '74. I think that I was elected easily that time because I had nine years' worth of practicing lawyers whom I'd taught now out in the workforce, plus all of those former students from law school at Alabama who had used my study notes over the years. Lawyers, at least, knew who I was and the name recognition among the voters made a world of difference.

What Made Janie Run?

Arden: Why did you want to be a Supreme Court justice?

Janie: I clerked for a long time, and that involved similar types of detail research. I might have been the only one of the bunch who liked the actual work. Much of the work consisted of research and writing persuasively, at least persuasively enough to attract four votes from fellow Supreme Court judges.

It is not for everybody. It's a solitary life in one sense. Your buddies don't come in to talk with you all day long and you don't talk about the cases with your lawyer friends. But I found it extremely challenging. I loved the professional camaraderie on the court. You could fall out with somebody, but we stayed comrades because we were mutually dependent in many ways for the bigger good of the institution; and it just suited my temperament somehow.

Arden: When did you make the decision and why?

Janie: I made the decision for the purely pragmatic political standpoint, believing I had as much chance as anybody. We hadn't had real elections for judges in many years since incumbents running for re-election seldom had opposition. I seemed just as apt to get elected as anybody else so it wasn't a hard decision for me from a pragmatic standpoint.

Arden: From a personal standpoint, when you started law school, did you always want to be a judge?

Janie: Heavens, no!

Arden: So, what drew you ?

Janie: I think the work itself suited my niche in the mental department. You know, it's just kind of fun to find what the law is and apply it to these facts, just on a purely "don't know any of the parties and don't care" basis. You know, I hadn't come from that in-crowd world where it's your old friends who are litigating and so on. So I was about as pure as you could get with a purely academic approach to the cases.

As I said, I liked the work. A lot of them didn't, at all. You can imagine it's not easy for some people to write. Many could easily decide the cases, knew where the case had to go, but to sit down and write an opinion justifying that, and supporting it with some authority, using logic, common sense – it's a lot harder than just calling strikes and balls.

Arden: How did your family feel about your running for judge?

Janie: They thought that I must have lost my mind. You know, my God in heaven, you mean you have to go everywhere in the state of Alabama and ask for votes just like you were running for governor? That's how big the territory is, and they just couldn't imagine my doing it. But they were enthusiastic about it anyway. They put signs on their cars. John went to his hunting camps where he hunted turkeys every year, and got every vote he could there. Willie did the same thing. She called her friends, got out and helped.

Arden: What about Jim and your daughter Laura?

Janie: Laura was too little; she wasn't involved much. And I made a decision. I certainly did not want Jim campaigning with me. I mean, there was no need to attract his enemies. I was always concerned about the race issue negatively affecting people in the campaign. To say the name Shores was a negative in some quarters because of my stance on Civil Rights. So Jim didn't politic with me at all.

I had no money at all, couldn't think of doing television ads; that's way too expensive, but I went all over the state, meeting with editorial boards of the newspapers. My friend, Annette Dodd, who had been John David's friend, did campaign with me. We'd stop at every radio station. When we saw a radio tower, we'd just go in and introduce ourselves, and they would put me on the air. Annette was especially good at this. She would announce to whoever was there (usually a lone disc jockey playing records and filling time between them) that I was running for the Alabama Supreme Court and she'd make it sound like the most important position in the world. The response was amazing! They most always played records and talked to us in between. They were almost without exception nice to us and welcomed us to town -- just fun.

My campaign consisted largely of lawyer endorsements, editorial endorsements, and radio. I found that you could get people to cut statement tapes for you, and send the tapes to the radio stations, and they'd play them. So we would often ask lawyers in a town to make a tape supporting me and send it to the local station. It was not difficult and it was effective.

You can get quite a lot of mileage off a long trip to a little town. In almost all of these little towns, I guess there still are radio stations, but you don't think about it much anymore from the standpoint of a statewide race since television has become so universal.

The High Price of Office

I forget how much I spent in the '72 race but not much for a campaign. On the one I won in '74, I spent $34,000 total. In comparison, judicial candidates in the most recent election here in Alabama spent about $8 million collectively.

When I ran for a position on the court, only the lawyers were particularly interested in the elections. Judges are supposed to operate beyond politics with rational consideration only for the legality of the issues. Now judicial elections are run like any other emotional political race. It's gotten to be awful.

In 1998 I decided reluctantly not to run for another term, and the cost of campaigns had a lot to do with it. Howell Heflin and his advice had a lot to do with my decision not to run. He was in the United States Senate, but retained his interest in court races. He made a point of talking to me about running again. He said he thought I probably could win, but wanted me to think about it. He first said, "You've got a wonderful record. It's going to be brutal this time; going to cost a lot of money. This race won't be like the last one. Why don't you just take a well-deserved vacation from the law and just not run again?" I told him that I would think about it.

Reneau Almon, who'd been elected at the same time I was, had already decided he wasn't going to run. Then Howell came back to talk to me again and told me Karl Rove was gearing up to come to Alabama to concentrate on judicial races, and that he would be well-heeled and mean. And he was. He moved to Montgomery and selected and supported the candidates that year, Republicans all. He ran campaigns and won those seats that were up that time, there were three of them.

Arden: When Senator Heflin said it was going to be brutal for you to run, did he mean on a personal level because of your liberal record that the opposition would be after you, or what?

Republican Effort to Eliminate Jury Trial

Janie: By that time, there was a group making a national effort to reform the civil justice system. The Chamber of Commerce, insurance companies, and the Karl Roves of the country had made "tort reform" words that people hadn't heretofore known. Most people didn't know what a tort was, much less that it needed reforming. But they knew that its "reform" was something that I was against and so they were probably for. So, yes, you could have gone through my voting record in the cases, and so on, and make an argument that I am on the side, normally, of upholding jury verdicts. And I am, and I did, and I'm unapologetic about it.

The Chamber of Commerce and the tort reformers continued to have as their quest the elimination of jury trials in civil cases. They may be successful, maybe not in my lifetime, but they will probably be in Laura's lifetime. We're the only major country on earth that has juries in civil cases; did you know that? We are. And as you see after the large settlements in favor of the people against the corporation in the Exxon cases, and others, the effort to eliminate juries in civil cases has become relentless.

There is an effort to protect big businesses from large penalties when juries find them negligent. There are mandatory arbitration clauses appearing now in every commercial contract. This is part of an effort to remove uncertainty and risk for big business. And I fear that they will win. This would be a serious loss of rights for individual Americans.

It's part of our American culture that the jury trial in civil cases cannot be eliminated. The Constitution says the right to a trial by jury shall remain inviolate. Now, if that doesn't mean you can't legislate it away, I don't know what does.

Jury Trial on Trial

You're told in law school right in the beginning that due process, as referenced in the Constitution, guarantees one the right to procedural due process. This means what it says: the justice system has to give a fair trial; the parties have a right to demand a jury to determine the facts, and the jury assesses damages based upon the evidence. This system has served us admirably, but in recent years the assault on the system has been relentless. Normally, they would say that you've got all the process you're due when the jury decides it, and the jury's been selected appropriately and there's no bias, and you can't find anything wrong with the process. If you lose your case, that's the end.

However, recently the Supreme Court of the United States has said that one has the right to some notion as to what range of damages might be awarded in a pending lawsuit. It used to say that a fair jury was all we're guaranteed under the Constitution, that no, we can't say exactly how much money is possible in a given case, but we can tell when it's an amount beyond what is allowed. That comes right after saying that the Supreme Court doesn't decide political questions. *Bush v. Gore* is a good example of that.

The court has held recently that a jury verdict in a civil case can be so excessive as to violate the due process clause of the U.S. Constitution. I think that notion was expressed in one of those automobile cases where the seller said the car was new, but it wasn't, said it hadn't been wrecked, and it had, and the jury gave a big verdict, I forget in what amount. The Supreme Court reversed the case saying that the amount exceeded what is allowed under the Due Process Clause. The Court did not say what amount would be constitutional. That's the kind of change to basic law that makes me really, really nervous.

Arden: You mean, the use of vague premises such as, "When I see it, I'll know it"?

Janie: Yes that "standard" was expressed by one of the justices in some of the early pornography cases. He was making the point that while it might be impossible to express a universal definition of speech not entitled to constitutional protection, that did not mean that it did not exist. He was merely saying that while one may not be able to define pornography legally, speech lost constitutional protection when it reached that point. In reviewing those cases, state courts had to make independent decisions as to whether or not it was permissible to ban movies and other material.

In my court, when we had a case involving a ban on a film on the grounds that it was pornographic and thus not entitled to protections under the Constitution, I sometimes would joke, "I don't have to go see that film. I want Hugh to go and Reneau to go, and both come back and tell me what you think, and then I'll know how to vote." I was saying this to show that it's inappropriate to decide constitutional issues based upon individual personal reaction. Judges are supposed to base their rulings on U.S. law even if it differs from their personal ideas.

How we decide - using subjective opinions vs. legal rules – is a serious question. This is a key issue that can diminish the civil rights of all citizens and make them powerless to appeal to the courts for justice. This legal basis for court decisions is part of what makes the United States a fairer country for citizens than anywhere else in the world. The rule of law and the court system is at the core of protecting people's rights. I think that if the people of America lose faith in the court system, if they come to believe that there's no fairness to be had there, then that's the end of our experiment in democracy.

As bad as it's gotten from time to time, even the blacks believed that they could get a fair shake in the Federal court system. They never lost that hope, and let's hope they never do because it would just be awful. That's why I'm so zealous about keeping any taint of diminishing people's rights or other basic changes to the rule of law away from the court system itself.

Rule of Law vs. Rule of Personal Opinion

That's why I hate it when the issue of civil court punitive damages awards is dismissed with some opinion like, "Oh, everybody knows that verdict is ridiculous. That's too much money to award someone." At least under our basic legal system, to set aside a jury verdict and modify its decision on damages, the trial judge has to go through the motions of explaining why the jury's decision on that issue is erroneous. A trial judge can't disregard a jury's decision on the damages awarded to an injured individual by merely saying something personal and vague like, "In this case, I think it's too much." I believe it entirely appropriate to require a court to state for the record a legitimate reason for substituting its judgment for that of the jury. I don't think people will accept a cavalier dismissal of the meaning of rights that are as fundamental as the right to trial by jury.

I can't imagine being able to retain any respect for yourself as a judge, if in your mind and heart you know that you really don't have a right under the law to second-guess a jury, but nevertheless to do so. When you take your oath as a lawyer or a judge, you swear to uphold the Constitution and the laws of the United States. You're not supposed to use your position as a soapbox to promote your individual opinions. You swear to promote, strengthen, and follow U.S. law, even if it varies from your personal preferences.

Maybe that's why I liked the law so much. The U.S. has a well-tested, well-thought-out legal system to protect citizens from the unpredictable whims of individuals. It allows citizens to know what rights and penalties they can expect from the courts. People, and especially lawyers and judges, should not use their personal opinions to decide cases and flip away our basic rights as though they don't mean anything. These legal safeguards help even the odds and protect the under-privileged. A U.S. citizen's access to the rule of law and trial by a jury of their peers is the fairest system so far devised by man.

Well, that's my Sermon on the Mount!

Just Call Me Janie

INTERVIEW III

PARENTS, PATRONS, & PREJUDICE

Arden: What did you do with the money that you earned as a child from your work after school?

Janie: I'm sure we were allowed to keep some, but we all just put it in together. You know, my mother, my sister, all of us, whatever we earned, it just went in one family pile.

We felt not at all deprived because all my friends handled things in much the same way. That was just the times in which we lived.

Arden: What kind of student were you?

Janie: I was a good student, without particularly trying to be. And Verla was, too. We were expected to do as well as we could. I'm sure I was probably in the top ten percent of my class academically, and Verla would have been, too; but again, that wasn't seen as remarkable at all. You were expected to do well.

Arden: Did your parents stress anything in particular? They expected you to do well. In what way would they have been disappointed?

Janie: How'd we get the message? I don't know, it certainly wasn't verbalized. You just knew that you were expected to do the right thing and would be frowned upon if you didn't. I don't remember ever getting into any trouble as a little kid.

Verla and I would sometimes speculate about not going directly home from school. We rode bicycles through the woods and not on heavily traveled roads, not that there were any really heavily traveled roads. But we were sometimes tempted to go play with somebody after school before going home because my mother wasn't there. Most often she'd be working anyway. But we almost never did, and if we did, we wouldn't stay long.

I don't know, we just had a subconscious desire not to make her upset or get her angry because she could get angry.

Arden: What happened when she got angry?

Janie: Send you to get the switch and then hit you with it.

Arden: What'd you do when you came home from school?

Janie: Depended on the time of year. If we had seasonal chores to do on the farm where we worked for the Marshalls, the potatoes, and so on, we'd do that.

We also had home chores assigned to us. Sometimes the chore would be to start supper, and mother would tell us how to do that. Always we were required to make sure our rooms were cleaned up and neat before we left for school. But, if not, it was supposed to be done as soon as we got home. We'd help clean the house.

Arden: Did you and Verla have separate rooms?

Janie: Yes. By the time we moved from Georgiana to Loxley and John was off to war, Verla and I had separate rooms. Until then we had shared a room. She and I were close. We were "us against them" mostly. We didn't mean to upset our parents or invade their privacy, but we could hear them talking because the house was so small. You could hear everything, and I have memories of hearing them talking with each other.

Banks & Mortgages are Bad

Sometimes I heard them discussing things I didn't really understand, but I could tell from their voices that they were talking about something terribly serious even though I didn't understand exactly what it was. By hearing them talk, I learned that a mortgage was a bad thing. Nobody should ever have a mortgage.

I got the impression that their regard for banks was quite low. This had to have been in the mid to late '30s. I would love to have been able to hear my dad John's reaction to the financial crisis we have just been through today. He would have been vindicated in his opinion of banks.

I could hear them talking about how things would be when John went off to war. They were worrying about that and how we would get along once that happened. There was a sense of urgency, a sense that time was running out, and we have to get ready, for this war is imminent.

They talked about rationing. There would be many types of goods that we couldn't get. And, of course, there were things that one could no longer get. One had to have stamps to buy gas. Butter was replaced with white oleomargarine that came with a little package of something yellow to be mixed with it to make it look like butter. It did not make it taste like butter, though.

Once the war was underway, tires became unavailable, so people didn't drive any more than they had to because gas was scarce, and car parts could not easily be replaced, etc.

Not long after we were settled in Loxley, and after working for a while in Mobile at the Alabama Dry Dock & Shipbuilding Company, John did go to the war. He had joined the Navy to avoid being drafted into the Army, Willie said.

Before he left they were talking about all of the things that should be considered in anticipation of his departure. Things like where we were going to live. You know you have to be somewhere. I'm sure this discussion about a mortgage was in connection with that; for example, if we bought a house, we'd have to have a mortgage, and that brought concerns about the risks involved.

Looking back, I don't think that there was any great likelihood that they would have even tried to buy a house then. But they discussed it. We rented a house until the war was over and he came back. Then they immediately bought a house and continued to talk about mortgages. I heard enough to understand that mortgages were bad, that interest payments were bad, and that banks were not on the same side as those seeking a mortgage.

I think they were on to something. A lifetime of experience has done little to change my view that banks, mortgages, interest, etc., should be regarded cautiously. Verla has spent her working life in the mortgage lending business, so she might not share my views on this.

Let's go back to our childhood relationship with John and Willie. As we were growing up, particularly when we were quite young, we were close to them in a way, but there was very little direct conversation. There was certainly no counseling us about such things as, here's what you must do to prepare yourself for the rest of your life. None of that.

I don't remember any discussion about our having to get a job. We had always had jobs, from working alongside Willie picking strawberries when we were still in grammar school, to picking up potatoes when we were in grade school, to working on the potato shed when we were in high school.

It was only natural, without a conversation being necessary upon graduating from high school, actually before graduating, that I started looking for a job. The word "college" had never been mentioned, I was delighted to get the first job I was interviewed for, just before I graduated. It was 1950, in the spring, and it might have taken weeks or months before I could find a job. But it was immediate. I took that as a good omen. Absolutely.

Arden: Do you have a fond memory of your father and a fond memory of your mom that stand out?

Janie: My dad was always the happiest and most talkative when he was around his family, mostly his brother, I guess; although his brother, Hollis, was much younger and talked all of the time. He still does.

Their father, my grandfather, was much revered by the grandchildren and by his own children as well. He didn't talk much either but when he did his children paid attention. He was a strong-willed man, I thought. He seemed to like Verla more than he did me, but that was all right. I know she liked him more than I did.

As for John and his siblings, there were six of them: Inez, Olga, John, Laura, Wynona, and the youngest, Hollis. We socialized mostly with them and their children, our cousins. Our family gatherings were quite festive and often included sage advice, mostly from the patriarch Steve.

The Mystery of Disappearing Steve

One day, the unchallenged family leader Steve left home without a word to anyone. His youngest child Hollis was about 15. Steve just got in his truck one day and drove off, without a word to anybody. Hollis claimed in later years that Steve did stop on his way down the driveway and give him $20 with the admonition to be sure to get a college education. But we all knew that was just one of Hollis's lies.

However, it is no lie that once it dawned on everybody that Steve was not coming back, his abandonment of the family dominated all conversation. I remember each one pledging not ever to have anything more to do with him if he did show back up. And of course, he eventually did. Not show back up, but his whereabouts were discovered a few years later. It turned out he had left with a woman who lived nearby. I don't remember her family name but her first name was Viola.

Someone, not a family member but one who knew the family, somehow learned that he was living in Plant City, Florida with Viola. A family caucus was called, and all of the children pledged never to seek him out or speak to him again if he ever showed up.

Inez was the first to break this pledge. After a while, maybe even years, she went to Plant City to see him, made peace with him, and eventually moved there with her husband, our Uncle Macy. They stayed several years.

I don't think any of the other children ever went so far as to visit with him, but even John agreed to meet with him many years later when he came back to Alabama to visit with, of course, Aunt Inez. I can't recall why, but years later Verla and I drove down to Plant City to visit with him. I even went to his funeral down there years after that.

Girls Don't Hunt

Growing up there were lots of family gatherings at my grandmother Trudy's house on weekends. This was John's mother, Gertrude King, but Trudy to everybody. Trudy grew up in Butler County. She had a brother named Marcus King whom I remember as being kind to us children. He was a bit aristocratic too, but that tone was probably demanded by his wife, our Aunt DeMoville, who was definitely aristocratic.

I remember those occasions at Trudy's as being very happy, festive even, with lots of cousins about, plus Hollis, who was not much older than the rest of us, but who took advantage of his senior status in every possible way. He usually had assignments for us that benefitted him in the form of work on some project that he was either supposed to do or wanted done.

We spent many summer weeks building a camp for all of us to use when we were there. After it was finished, he declared it off limits to us. He did the same thing with bird traps.

He knew how to build a trap and could catch birds when they came in to eat cracked corn that he baited it with. Only he could get the birds out. Sometimes he let them go, but when they were partridges, he gave them to Granny to cook for him, and only for him.

Both John and Hollis had great love for turkey hunting. Later on, they went deer hunting, although they never cared very much for that. Both of them loved to turkey hunt, and John did so until he was well into his 80s. Hollis, now in his 80s, still does.

Arden: Did he teach you to hunt?

Janie: No. Girls didn't go hunting.

Arden: That was the message that you got, girls don't go hunting?

Janie: Yes, they didn't. Now, he would take us fishing from time to time, even when we were quite little. He'd take us down to the Gulf, or sometimes to the Bon Secour River, especially in the wintertime. I guess fishing was all right for girls.

Baby chickens were another activity in which girls were included. My mother ordered baby chickens that would come from somewhere chirping in a box in the mail.

I always picked one out to be my personal chicken, taking care of it and petting it, but I don't believe chickens can make friends with people. I never noticed that my chicken acted any differently than the others.

One of our chores was to feed the chickens and to gather the eggs. The chickens would come as these little yellow babies, and you could feed those chickens every day, and pet them, and pick one out to be your pet. They never knew you. No, chickens have no loyalty, no ability to bond at all.

I don't know how much this annual rite of ordering baby chickens was based upon economics and how much of it was because she found it fun and satisfying to raise them. I don't think we had enough for her to be doing it as a way to make money. I don't remember her selling eggs, for example.

Arden: Did she sell the chickens?

Janie: No, I don't think so. I don't remember her selling chickens. But I remember I got into eggs, and sometimes keeping certain ones that she would mark, and later she'd hatch them, too; rather than buying the little ones, she'd hatch them by herself.

Arden: What would she do with all those little chicks?

Janie: They grew up and made eggs.

Arden: What was your school like?

Janie: I liked school. I wanted to go to the first grade with my cousin Lucy, who was one year older than me, but I had to wait another year.

From the first grade through the second, I went to school in Georgiana. I can remember the smell. It was a new, red brick building, and they oiled or waxed the floors. It was slippery. It had a distinctive smell that I continue to associate with the first grade.

After the third grade, I went to Loxley Elementary that included grades one through nine, except for one year, the eighth grade; that year Verla and I went to Daphne School. This came about because my mother took a job in Spanish Fort, which is not far from Loxley but it's in a different school district. My father was still in the Navy, serving in the Pacific.

After he came back, we moved back to Loxley, but we had an enjoyable year living in Spanish Fort and going to Daphne School.

Robertsdale's One Unlisted Number

From the ninth grade on through twelfth, we went to Robertsdale High School, as did students from communities all around. It was a so-called consolidated high school, where students from Loxley, Rosinton, Summerdale, Silverhill, etc., all the little towns around Robertsdale, would go.

Tim Cook, now the CEO of Apple, is probably our most famous alumnus or at least our most successful one. His family still lives in Robertsdale and folks say he calls them every Sunday. Someone recently told me that his family had the only unlisted phone number in the county.

Multi-Cultural Country Life

Our high school, looking back, was very diverse in terms of ethnicity. Silverhill is made up largely of people from Eastern Europe: Poland, Yugoslavia, Czechoslovakia, etc. In fact, Baldwin County remains one of the most diverse counties in Alabama. Germans settled in Elberta and Robertsdale. Greeks settled in Malbis and Italians in Daphne.

Those neighborhoods still retain their ethnic identities to this day. Some of the most prosperous citizens in Baldwin County come from those immigrant farmers who were extremely successful.

The Cortes were Italian. They were very successful farmers and developed beautiful land and created beautiful estates. The Bertollas were another Italian family that became successful. Some of the descendants of these early immigrants are still farming. I saw Freddie Corte the other day. He has the most gorgeous farm you've ever seen, just wonderful. And the retention of their cultural traditions was interesting.

As children, we never knew anything about any kind of prejudice in terms of ethnicity. We always had great admiration for the work ethic of the Italian farmers. The Greeks at Malbis were highly successful in the bakery business. They, to this day, welcome any Greek immigrant who shows up in Baldwin County. The Greeks built beautiful buildings. The architecture in Malbis is stunning. The early settlers built a beautiful Greek Orthodox Church that is still there. It was a wonderful tradition: any Greek who came to this part of the world had a home there as long as they needed it.

I didn't know anything about prejudice of any sort until I got to the University of Alabama. Of course, this acceptance of immigrants did not include black people, but even there I don't recall any overt prejudice. They simply were ignored except for domestic help whom we knew personally.

As meager as our resources were, for much of our childhood we had a cleaning woman most of the time. We were taught – no, threatened – never to use the word "nigger." And we never did and seldom heard it used by others. All of that was to come much later.

I became aware of racial prejudice for the first time at the University. I had a friend who was Lebanese, and one of my friends from Mobile, seeing me studying with him, whispered to me, "You know he's Lebanese, don't you?" Well, no, I didn't, and I didn't know why that was significant. No, we simply didn't have that, at all, that I ever experienced in Baldwin County.

We did have a store in Loxley that people said was run by a Jew. His name was Jake. Another store was run by a Greek man, George Marinus. People traded with them without any reservation. I think there was much more awareness of ethnicity in Mobile, but then Mobile was much more socially conscious than we were in rural Baldwin County. I think Mobilians looked down on everybody from Baldwin County. Many of them had summer cottages "over the bay" but otherwise only passed through Baldwin County.

I would say that our childhood was as nearly perfect as it could have been without any affluence whatsoever. Of course, there were families who were a bit better off than we were, I am sure, but it was not a matter of concern. It seemed to me that we were all about the same. Certainly the ones whose families had big farms worked just as much as we did.

Verla used to say that she thought anybody who lived in a brick house must be rich. I suppose she thought this because most of the houses were almost always wood houses, many made of cypress because for a long time it was so plentiful. There were the large areas of cypress swamps where the trees grew all through south Alabama. Cypress wood makes pretty houses, and it ages beautifully. Rather like New England hues, although down here cypress turns a different grayish color with the aging process.

You asked me about finding a job in Mobile and how that changed my life. I rode the Greyhound bus every morning, and came back every afternoon. Most of the passengers were people like me who were going into Mobile for jobs.

Grade School Expectations

Arden: When you got a job, what did you think you were expected to do before the influence of Mr. Kilborn and your exposure to other options; what was your vision of your life to come? Did you have a thought about how your life was going to progress?

Janie: I don't recall dwelling on it at all. I had some things that I thought you were supposed to avoid at all costs. One was, don't drop out of school. You stayed until you graduated from high school.

Do not get married before you get out of school. And it goes without saying: do not get pregnant, before or after. Because I think that people, particularly my mother, looked on that as it just dooms you if you get married before you get an education. It's just the end of all hope. That was my impression, at any rate. Although it seemed to me that she and John, who got married when they were very young, never regretted having done so.

Arden: That's interesting that you don't remember discussions about college or anything, but your mom was emphatic about marriage, pregnancy and finishing school. What did you feel that she wanted you to do instead of marrying young?

Janie: Anything other than that. She would express it when we heard that some classmate was getting married, which was a common occurrence. She was not very verbal but she expressed such obvious disappointment, sadness even, without verbalizing it, and it was unmistakable. We got that message loud and clear.

Arden: Did you get any message about what the alternative was?

Janie: We would be applauded to get a job. That was excellent news, welcome news. And we both did.

Verla graduated the next year and she also got a job in a law office. Her lawyer boss pretty soon became a bankruptcy judge, and she went with him to his new job and stayed with him a long time. His name was Sidney Gray.

I stayed with Kilborn for almost four years. He didn't encourage me to go to law school; he just suggested that I had a good sense of the law, which was the first time I'd ever dreamed that it might even be a possibility. So I started thinking about it. And I soon learned that you've first got to go to college.

Arden: How old were you when you first got married?

Janie: Nineteen, I think. Bill Ellzey's father had bought him a grocery store in Loxley. I don't know why that would have occurred. I wish I'd asked more about it. I had the impression that both of them wanted Bill to do something before he worked in the family gravel business.

By the time we got married, it was settled that he was going back to Selma to go into the family business with his dad. I agreed to move to Selma with the understanding that I would go to college and then to law school when we got to Selma.

The University of Alabama at that time offered classes around various towns, including Selma. I took all I could take there, and then I went over to Marion about thirty miles away to Judson College, a Baptist-affiliated, all girls' college. I took as many hours as I could each semester, having learned that the University of Alabama would permit one to enter law school upon the completion of ninety hours in undergraduate school. The last thirty of those hours, however, had to be earned on campus.

That's the reason I had to go to Tuscaloosa before entering law school. I completed that work and entered law school in the second semester, in February 1956. I now have an anomaly. I graduated from law school in 1959 and from undergraduate school in 1968. For the next fifty years, people just assumed that the unusual dates were typographical errors.

Many of the students were mature people who were involved in whatever careers they were in, who couldn't have gone to law school otherwise, but could now that there was a full-time law school in Birmingham. We did have a night law school in Birmingham, and still do, but the prospect of having an accredited one was attractive to people as a foundation for a second career.

Reneau Almon, for example, who later served with me on the Alabama Supreme Court, was working at Redstone Arsenal in engineering, having graduated from the University of Alabama in business and engineering. He resumed his education and went to law school.

The Pleasure of Teaching

I joined the faculty in 1966. I was working at Liberty National, in the legal department there, when Dean Weeks called and asked me to come and teach. My daughter Laura was born in 1964 so she was two. The teaching schedule was extremely attractive to me in terms of hours and flexibility.

I had good help with her at home, and Liberty National had been very generous in their treatment of me. They gave me a pregnancy leave, the first one they ever gave anybody, when Laura was born. So it was not a great burden to me to have a nine-to-five job; but even so, teaching was attractive to me for several reasons, and one of them was being able to adjust my time to be available to attend her.

The student body was small; the faculty was small; the law school was new to the area; so the faculty cooperated and selected courses that we found especially interesting until we settled on subjects we really liked and wanted to really get into and become somewhat expert in. We all taught nearly every subject for a time. Of course, some came in as experts. My friend from high school, Claude Bankester, had a LLM in tax law and came to the faculty as our tax professor.

After some switching around, I settled into teaching Constitutional Law, Conflict of Laws, and some Practice and Procedure. My years of writing pleadings dictated by Vincent Kilborn were very helpful in learning and teaching.

Mobile was among the last counties in Alabama to adopt "code pleading" based upon the federal rules of civil procedure. It retained the old common law pleading that most law students found perplexing. The legislature of Alabama passed the Rules of Civil Procedure for the State of Alabama sometime in the '60s after I got out of law school, so law students in my time had to learn both.

My training with Mr. Kilborn was invaluable to me in understanding and being able to teach the pleading in procedure courses. So much so that I found myself getting tired of those, so I taught Constitutional Law several years, and then finally wound up teaching Conflict of Laws as well.

Conflict of Laws was my favorite course because it enabled me to get a sense of what grasp the student had of the whole judicial picture. Certainly it was true of my classmates and later on my students, that many of us were especially challenged by this course. It is called "conflict of laws" because the law of more than one jurisdiction is involved.

A lawsuit can be brought in any state where service of process over the defendant can be perfected. The law of the forum, however, controls. That law often calls for the application of the law of the state, for example, where the cause of action arose, or, in another context, where the contract sued upon was created. The law of the forum includes that state's conflict of laws rule, which often requires the application of the law of another state. A state's conflict of laws rule is applicable in any kind of litigation. The conflict of laws rule of the forum state may or may not involve the application of the law of more than one state.

A judge trying a case must apply applicable law, and if properly raised, that includes the forum's conflict of laws rule that might require the application of the law of another jurisdiction.

I don't mean to give a lecture on the subject, but I mention this example only to illustrate why some students had trouble with this area of the law, which might explain why this became my favorite course to teach. It is a sophisticated body of law that's grown and created rules for dealing with the law of more than one jurisdiction.

Being with Bill

Arden: Tell me some more about Bill Ellzey.

Janie: Bill Ellzey was a sweet, gentle soul, not very bright, but not a mean bone in his body. Not very ambitious, but he didn't have to be very ambitious. Papa, I called him, his father, took care of all that. Papa was very protective of Bill.

I called him Bill, although his family continued to call him Billy Butler, which was his formal name. He came to Loxley right out of Auburn University. He had no connection to this area. I always assumed that he was trying to delay going into the family business for a while, although by every indication he did not resent going into it when he eventually did, and seemed to enjoy being there, working with his father.

Butler was his mother's maiden name, and she was called Billie. I think he was somewhat embarrassed to have been named for his mother, although he was devoted to her, and she adored him.

He suffered from epilepsy, petit mal it's called, and had since infancy. It was not especially debilitating when I met him and episodes didn't occur very often, certainly not after I knew him. I think as a child the seizures, the incidents, were more prevalent and more frequent than they later became.

In the eight or nine years we were married, I only saw three incidents of it. It would have been dangerous had he been driving a car since they came without warning. Fortunately, he was at home and simply became totally unconscious, began shaking uncontrollably, couldn't hear or speak. After it was over, he did not want to talk about it and I doubted that he was aware of what had happened.

I think this condition made his parents very protective and I got the impression that Bill wasn't expected to perform very well. I believe they always assured him that he shouldn't worry, that things will work out, everything will be taken care of. And they were. I always admired them for their efforts to give him a normal life.

I am not sure that he needed as much support as they gave him. He always had the newest car, often a convertible. I don't think the grocery store was considered a serious business.

Back working for his father in Selma was real work. They mined sand and gravel and made concrete pipe, and poured concrete in big trucks. Bill didn't know how to do any of that. I think he wrote up orders. I remember times when it seemed to me he would be required, if there were some big project going on, to be there if they had to make deliveries on weekends. Big concrete pipe, half as big as this room, had to be delivered for big construction projects. His job was not taxing, certainly not intellectually taxing, anyway.

Mr. Ellzey's Interests

As you can imagine, the success of the business had to have been the ability to bid on and get the big contracts, and lease the land, or acquire the mineral rights. Mr. Ellzey owned lots of land himself but acquired the mineral rights, or rights to sand and gravel on much more.

His business interests required him to be very active in local and state politics. One could not build roads in the county without what he produced; and one couldn't be successful in a competitive business that was closely tied to politics without participating in politics.

I've thought many times that his vehemently insisting upon supporting the White Citizens Council, and insisting that all of the family do so, had a significant business connection. When I said I'm not supporting it, I'm not being part of it, and you are not allowed to put my name on it as being a member of it, it infuriated him. I was as adamant about that issue as he was.

His words were, "Well, if that's the position you're taking, then I no longer consider you a part of this family." And I no longer considered myself part of the family. And poor Bill didn't say a word. He just didn't take a position one way or the other.

Arden: How'd that make you feel?

Janie: It made me feel there's not but one solution, and so I announced: it's over. And I'm leaving. And I did. Poor Bill, I don't think he ever, ever had anything at all to say. He accepted without question his father's decision, and I prepared to leave Selma.

Arden: All the discussions about the divorce were between you and his father?

Janie: Bill and I worked it out, or more accurately, there was little to work out. I didn't want anything from him. We didn't have much money and I didn't think he owed me anything. We had a house, which we built. There was a mortgage on it, and I had my law office, and a small practice, not worth much.

I suggested that in exchange for my interest in the house, Bill assign his life insurance policy to me. It was not a big policy, but my thinking was that it was an asset against which I could borrow some money if I needed to.

I remembered what I had been told by the bank president when I leased my law office in the new bank building, and explained that although I didn't have any money at all, I had pretty good prospects and thought I could attract enough clients to pay the rent.

He kept looking at the figures I was giving him, and just as grim as could be, he said, "Janie, you're seriously undercapitalized."

I thought about that when I was leaving Selma. I still think about it. I definitely was undercapitalized as I left Selma, but that was hardly a consideration. At that time, I didn't want to spend more time negotiating. I just wanted to leave.

So I agreed to deed my interest in the house to Bill while continuing to bear the obligation on the lease of the office. I suggested that he assign his life insurance policy to me, which would give me an asset in the cash value of the policy. I suggested he could designate anyone he wanted as beneficiary.

I made this suggestion as a way to avoid any financial obligation on his part and as a way to compensate me for my interest in the house. He agreed. Bill would own the house. I would relinquish all interest in it and in exchange I would own the policy, but no money was involved.

It was a poor bargain for my side, but I thought it was more than fair to Bill. He thought so, too. I wanted at least a little capital as I set off alone.

So that was our agreement.

We agreed to file the divorce petition in Baldwin County. So, with all of the documents signed, I went down to file them. I had barely arrived at my mother's house, when Bill called to tell me not to file the divorce petition, saying that his father didn't like the agreement we had reached. I asked, "What more does he want? It can't get any more favorable to your side." Well, Bill said, "Dad doesn't like it, you owning the life insurance policy."

Arden: That's the only thing you wanted?

Janie: So, what did he propose instead of that? Bill said, "Well, he would just rather give you a note, payable monthly." I don't remember the amount, but it was not more than $10,000 (my interest in the house was worth much, much more) but Mr. Ellzey wanted Bill's obligation to me fixed and he suggested a note payable monthly until paid in full.

I had no objection to this and in fact it was much more favorable to me than the arrangement I had suggested. So that's what we did, and I don't remember how much, but it was all paid off in a couple of years, so it couldn't have been much. But that was all right. I didn't want much. I felt guilty enough having, subliminally, known that the chance to go to college was the most attractive part of getting married to start with.

Arden: Why did you marry him? He obviously wasn't your intellectual equal.

Janie: No, but, selfishly, I couldn't figure out a way to go to college without some sort of income. However, when I got to Selma, I went to work right away anyway; I got a job out at Craig Air Force Base. I was a secretary again, for some colonel.

Arden: Still that work ethic!

Janie: Yes, you know, I just felt trifling sorry when I didn't have a job.

Arden: So, the breakup of your marriage was not really emotional?

Janie: No, it was hard, but it was a breach beyond an emotional one. There was just no compromising our beliefs on either side. I thought that leaving was the most honest thing I could do.

Arden: To you, it may have been more about divorcing his family than just Bill because he was a nice man.

Janie: Yes, he was.

Divorcing Selma

I couldn't imagine remaining in Selma with this major disagreement, and everyone knew that tensions were going to get worse. We had moved there in 1953 or 1954. *Brown v. The Board of Education* was decided in 1954 in the summer. The impact of that decision dominated every conversation.

I don't remember a single person who took the position that the decision should be followed and that efforts should commence to peacefully integrate the schools. To the contrary, every conversation centered on the commitment to keep the schools segregated. Some were more aggressive in how that would be accomplished. Some argued that public schools should simply be closed.

Some people believed that the "colored" people were just as unhappy as they were and doubted that they would attempt to go to white schools. Others believed that the schools should be kept just as they were and expressed a willingness to do whatever was necessary to assure that they were. I don't remember any argument in favor of the decision.

I tried to avoid the subject, but that was not possible. Selma was segregated in every way, but so was the remainder of the South. Everybody I knew was kind to their "help" and treated them kindly. I didn't know anyone who would have suggested that whites were inherently superior, but there was seemingly universal agreement that it was best for everybody to keep the schools "separate but equal."

Interestingly, almost everybody we knew had domestic help who were black. As poor as my family was, we had Helen, who worked for us while Verla and I were growing up. My grandmother, John's mother, had Miraha. They helped with the housework and with the laundry, mostly ironing. I don't remember any feeling that we were superior to Helen. It was more a sense that we're all in this together.

That wasn't the way it was in Selma, although the Ellzeys couldn't have been nicer to the help they had. They were extremely nice to them, and I think they were genuinely fond of them. But as I was to learn when the effort to organize and form the White Citizens Council got under way, that did not prevent otherwise nice people from endorsing and promoting unbelievably harsh ideas.

Mr. Ellzey seemingly thought there was nothing unreasonable in requiring our domestic help to disclose every meeting they held with other 'colored people,' as we referred to them then. If they were having a meeting at a black church, they were expected to tell their employers when, where, and what it was about. They were expected to report what had taken place there, who came, what was said.

When I asked what this Citizens Council was going to do with this information, his response was general: "We're going to keep up with what the black people are doing." Well, you say if they're going to a meeting, they have to tell their employer where they're going. Does that mean they have to get permission to go? My questions made him furious but they did not change his mind.

The White Citizens' planning meetings continued, but I was not welcome anymore after I expressed my distress with the entire subject. The meetings included some of the most prominent members of the town and some of the elected officials. Jim Clark, the Sheriff of Dallas County, was a prominent member. So was the local state senator. They were all very active in planning ways to preserve what I think they truly believed was a system which was right.

Arden: They were organizing it at Papa Ellzey's house?

Janie: Yes. And others' houses, too.

Arden: And dividing up the territory?

Janie: Making the plans about how it was going to work. Literally. And I didn't hear nearly all of it. But it was as if the black people were going to have to tell their employers when they were going to any kind of gathering, church, whatever it is, they had to know when they were getting together as a group.

Now, there's something in my background that just couldn't accept that. My parents did not talk much about anything but they did teach me morals, and I learned a clear difference between right and wrong. I just couldn't imagine pretending that the racism was all right because it wasn't all right.

The Invisible Line

Many people did unfair or racist things anyway. They often would protest that, "We paid them more generously than we had to, and we paid them for every service they ever rendered." And, yes, they had. In many ways, certainly with the ones who worked for them, those white people treated colored people generously and kindly. They would assist their help's family when a child was sick. They would help when a family member got in trouble. They did not personally overtly mistreat them. Yet there seemed to be a line that was inalterable. As long as no one breached the line, everything was all right; but the line was drawn and it was non-negotiable.

There's not much difference now. Things are better now, but there is still a line, and it's still rarely discussed openly.

For the most part, public schools in the South are still not integrated. There are a few black children in a few public schools attended by both races, but for the most part white people have abandoned public schools. They go by different names, but there are "academies" all over the South that came about as a result of the decision in *Brown v. Board of Education*. Two men wrote a fine book about that called the *Schools that Fear Built* (David Nevin and Robert E. Bills, Introduction by Terry Sanford, President, Duke University).

Many public schools have been abandoned by white people. Many people simply took their children out of the public schools and put them often in religious academies in the same neighborhoods. This movement of white flight from public schools has not abated so far as I can tell.

I think we have a fairly good public school system in this county and I know that the Mountain Brook School System near Birmingham is one of the best public systems still standing. But it existed before *Brown*. Mountain Brook, the city, village really, was founded in the early part of the 20th century to avoid the coarseness of the coal-mining settlement Birmingham. Now, all of these years later, Birmingham has not recovered from that white flight

Watching people preparing to resist integration of the schools in Selma, I was often perplexed. For the most part, these were kind people, people who had done a lot to ease the lives of, if not all, at least "their" colored people. Yet they simply could not imagine sending their children to the same school.

This fear and determination were expressed in different ways. Most espoused the political principle of "separate but equal." Others agreed with George Wallace who preached

"Segregation now. Segregation forever." When the subject was calmly discussed -- and it seldom was -- a real fear was discernible. It was a fear of what integration, over time, might lead to. The George Wallace followers called it *mongrelization* of the races. Others used less inflammatory language, but the fear of losing the distinctions between black and white was the same. It was as though everyone was preparing for a war.

Hardship & Heroes

The race was started for real with *Brown v. The Board of Education* federal decision for integrated schools in 1954. The next summer, Rosa Parks, a gentle seamstress in Montgomery sat down near the front of the city bus in Montgomery. She refused to move when the bus driver told her to. Police were called. She was taken to jail.

Rosa called Virginia Durr and her husband Clifford for help. Now this leads me into another digression.

I met Virginia through Paul Johnston who came to practice law with Jim after he fell into disfavor at his family firm for getting involved in the "unsavory civil rights mess." A classmate, then in the Kennedy administration, had asked him to help a man who had been arrested in connection with the death of Viola Liuzzio, who although from up North decided to join the voting rights marches in the South. The man arrested was an undercover agent for the government who had infiltrated the KKK.

Mrs. Durr Powders Her Nose

Virginia Durr and Clifford had spent many years in Washington. Clifford, like Virginia, was born into a patrician family He was a Rhodes Scholar and after law school joined a distinguished Birmingham law firm. He was fired after defending a secretary who had been fired. His brother-in-law, Hugo Black (married to Virginia's sister), encouraged him to come to Washington. Hugo was a Senator and Supreme Court Justice who had been a member of the KKK but changed his thinking and became a supporter of civil rights. Clifford did as Hugo urged him and gained a substantial position in the Roosevelt Administration.

Virginia Durr pursued her liberal causes and was eventually called before the Senate Committee investigating communists. She was a brave and colorful character. During the questioning at the McCarthy hearings, Virginia made a point to frequently open her compact and powder her nose to indicate that she was not cowed by the proceedings.

Back in Montgomery, the Durrs continued to support liberal causes and often opened their modest home for young civil rights supporters from out of town. I remember one of Bobby Kennedy's kids staying with them for weeks. It is not surprising that Rosa Parks, helped by activist E.D. Nixon, called the Durrs for help when she got arrested. Fred Gray, the first black Montgomery lawyer, later represented Rosa.

I saw quite a lot of Virginia after Clifford died. She had old friends in the area. One was Gould Beech, another old liberal. Virginia visited with me often.

Back to Montgomery. A young black preacher came to town as the minister at the Dexter Avenue Baptist Church. Along with other black leaders, he called for a boycott of the buses. As in many Southern towns, Montgomery city buses were mainly used by black people, not as a protest but because most white people had a car of some kind. Buses were the main means of transportation for black maids going to work for white families in the city suburbs.

The bus boycott was successful, but it also created a real nuisance for white people. Many of Montgomery's white housewives started car pools, taking turns going to black neighborhoods and bringing maids to work. That earned many of them disapproval from other whites who believed that integration of the races in schools, buses, lunch counters, etc., was the beginning of the end of the Southern way of life.

While all of this was going on, and tension was high, a voter registration effort was launched to register blacks. Although blacks in many counties accounted for more than fifty percent of the population, they accounted for less than ten percent of registered voters. Some leaders remarked, partly in jest, that too much worry was being expended on that issue, pointing out that women had been permitted to vote for a half century and that it had not made any difference.

The voter registration drive was undertaken seriously in Selma. Martin Luther King, Jr. and many of the national leaders of the "movement," as the cause would come to be called, came to help the registration efforts. They were met with resistance.

I remember black people being turned back as they attempted to enter the courthouse to register. The county sheriff and his deputies literally knocked them off of the steps of the courthouse, and many wound up in jail for failing to obey a law officer.

Had they made it inside the courthouse, they would have been asked to read and interpret various provisions of the Constitution. I remember when I registered the first time, I was asked to read a provision of the Constitution and explain its meaning to the person charged with handling the "government's work" that day. Neither my answer nor his understanding of the constitutional language bore any relationship to the document we were interpreting.

I didn't grasp the extent of the movement at the time, but no one could fail to notice that these different incidents were not random. Someone had given much thought to them, and being served at a dime store lunch counter or allowed to sit anywhere on a city bus was not going to be enough to satisfy what surely had to have been years of pent-up anger over an unjust way of life. The determination of the blacks was met with equal determination on the part of some white leaders to stop, or at least delay, any change to the "Southern way of life." All of the ingredients for violent eruptions were there. Of course, violence soon came.

I had left Selma before the famous march to Montgomery took place, but I was there when the conditions that led to the march were very much in place. A group of blacks set about to register black voters long before the actual march. There was a systematic effort by some white officials to prevent the registration of blacks to vote. I don't know the exact numbers but I am sure that blacks outnumbered whites in Dallas County and I am equally sure that only a small percentage of them were registered to vote.

The principal players in the 1965 March from Selma to Montgomery have now become familiar to most of us. Frank Johnson was the Presiding Judge of the United States District Court in Montgomery, a lifetime Republican who had been appointed by President Eisenhower. His law school classmate, George Wallace, was the governor, with bigger political ambitions. Lyndon Johnson was U.S. President. John Patterson had the Ku Klux Klan backing and was more anti-black than George Wallace had been during the 1958 race for governor. I supported Jimmy Faulkner in that race. Most of my friends worked for a liberal from Gadsden, George Hawkins, who was President Pro Tem of the Senate.

John Patterson was considered a dark horse. The only thing he had going for him was his daddy, a district attorney, had been killed down in Phenix City by gambling thugs in some conflict totally unrelated to race. It was gambling that took him, the gambling interests; this issue continues to haunt us.

John Patterson had the sympathy vote for the loss of his father, and George Wallace was beaten because Patterson ran on the anti-black issue. He won the governor's race on the race issue. I never shall forget the night of the primary, the first vote.

Sag Wallace

George C. Wallace kept his vow never to be "out-segged" in a political campaign again. And he never was. Racism and segregation became the core of his campaigns.

George's younger brother, Sag, as we called Gerald O. Wallace was a delightful, funny person and a friend. He'd been injured in the war, and I think I recall that he had had tuberculosis. He had a terrible scar that went all the way across his chest and around his back.

His closest friend and another classmate was Cecil Jackson. My friend, Cecil was from Selma and was often my co-counsel in appointed death cases at a time when we were both new lawyers in Selma. He also became George Wallace's legal advisor. Cecil had had polio, one of the last in that age group to contract it before the polio vaccine became widely available. He was very slight. He had to use braces and crutches all his life. He was very smart, but was physically just a bad-looking specimen.

Sag, for reasons not quite clear, designated me as one of his people to be called in an emergency. Not too often, but once a semester or so, he would have too much to drink and wind up in the hospital, mostly because he looked to be in such terrible straits that folks would get scared for him and take him to the hospital.

Don Patterson was another good friend of Sag's and mine. He too was on Sag's list of people designated to be called in case of emergency. Don later became a circuit judge in Florence. He was tall, blond, good looking, with a deep voice. He was one of those men with a voice that can't speak softly; it comes out loud no matter what.

During our senior year, Don and I got calls early one morning from the hospital telling us that Gerald Sag Wallace was in the hospital. We went to the hospital and when we found Sag, he looked perfectly dreadful. He was draped under a tent; they were giving him oxygen, I guessed. He looked to me to be close to terminal. I didn't know what to make of it, but found it awful. Don looked across at me and with that loud voice he said, "Oh, God, Janie, why weren't we nicer to him?"

Fortunately, Sag recovered and went on to live and thrive throughout George's repeated terms as governor. Whether he really was, as rumored, his brother's political bagman collecting proceeds from illicit deals and activities, I don't know. He was never formally charged with any criminal activity.

Kennedy in 1960

Arden: You told me another disagreement between you and your father-in-law arose out of the John Kennedy race in 1959-60. You and another woman opened an office for Kennedy in Selma, Alabama.

Janie: That's right.

Arden: And what kind of reception did you get?

Janie: Being ignored was the reception we got. Some black people would take our bumper stickers, but few whites showed any interest at all.

I did get a call from Earl Goodwin, State Senator and one of the leaders, toward the end. He said, "My God, it looks like your candidate may win." He didn't mean in Alabama, of course, but nationwide. It was a close Presidential race. In fact, they had to count votes twice in Chicago, I think. But it was interesting to see.

It was not a total wash in Alabama. Kennedy got at least some of the electoral votes, and that was due to John Patterson. Every time I get angry at John Patterson for being such a racist back in the '58 campaign, I remember that he relented and helped Kennedy some toward the end in the 60s.

Arden: Did you leave Selma right after that?

Janie: I was in Birmingham during the Democratic primary in the spring of 1962, when Jim Folsom showed up obviously intoxicated on television near Election Day. For that reason I think, he was defeated by George Wallace, who went on to be elected governor, the first of four times he would occupy that office. Wallace also ran for president four times.

Birmingham Battles

In Birmingham, I volunteered in Tom King's campaign when he was running for mayor. Once again, Birmingham had just had a brutal political battle over the race issue; it culminated in a change of the form of city government from a commission form to a mayor council form.

Bull Connor had long been the police commissioner and had drawn national attention to the racial strife starting in Birmingham. The situation was to get worse.

Art Hanes was the segregationist candidate. Tom King was running as a moderate, arguing that it was possible to make peace between the races. I volunteered to work in the Tom King campaign. It was there that I met Jim Shores, along with Chuck Morgan, Bob Vance, David Vann, and Peaches Taylor, among others, all young liberals who had worked diligently to change Birmingham. Most of them had also tried to ease racial tensions at the University when efforts to integrate the school had ended in violence.

Tom King had been administrative assistant to George Huddleston, the local congressman from Birmingham at the time. Tom King's father was a highly regarded circuit judge. The young Birmingham lawyers were enthusiastic about his chances of being elected mayor and excited about how that might change Birmingham. He was a good-looking, good clean candidate for first mayor under this new form of government. Things were looking hopeful until just before the election. Polls were showing a close race, but Tom clearly had a chance to win. Then, the picture was published.

Liberal Birmingham

Tom King was walking down the steps of City Hall just before election day, when a black man called out to him, then went up to him, and Tom shook his hand. An unseen photographer got a picture of the handshake, taken from inside City Hall. The photo appeared on the front page of the *Birmingham News* the next day. When the votes were counted, Tom King had lost — for shaking hands with a black man on the steps of the City Hall.

It was clearly a setback to those young liberals who were working hard for the future of the city. One side effect of these struggles was that through working in those campaigns, I met the brightest and most progressive young lawyers and other activists in Birmingham.

Arden: Were there many?

Janie: Well, Bob Vance, for many years was state chairman of the Democratic Party. He and his wife Helen became our best friends after I married Jim Shores. They became Laura's godparents some years later.

Chuck Morgan and Jim Shores were law partners. Tom King joined their firm after he lost the mayoral election. Peaches Taylor was a dear friend. He later served in the Peace Corps and wrote a constitution for one of the emerging nations of Africa. David Vann later became mayor himself.

Members of that group, supporters of Tom King's campaign, were the first people I met in Birmingham. Many of them became leaders of the liberal element in the political '60s.

Arden: Moving to Birmingham, did you have a job or did you plan to open an office?

Janie: I wasn't going to try to open an office because I had learned in Selma, where I did, that I was undercapitalized. One reason I volunteered in the King campaign was to spend some productive time while searching for a real job. I wanted to try for a Birmingham law firm in spite of prejudice against hiring women lawyers. I thought that the people working for the campaign would be able to give me some advice in that regard, some insight/ I planned to use the interval to job hunt. I met many nice people. Very few were from big law firms, but there were lots of young involved people who were very helpful.

I got word that Dean Harrison of Alabama Law School had suggested that I go see Mr. Arant of Bradley, Arant, Rose, and White, the oldest, biggest firm in Alabama. He was then president of the Birmingham bar or its immediate past president, and I think maybe president of the state bar association. In retrospect, it makes sense that Dean Harrison would suggest I seek his advice. I didn't question it. If Dean Harrison says I ought to do it, I ought to do it. I didn't want to do it, but I did it.

I went and I said, "Mr. Arant, Dean Harrison suggested that I come speak to you about finding a job in Birmingham." He seemed surprised at that. He said, "He did?" "Yes, sir." He said, "Well, let's see, have you interviewed the trust departments of the banks?" "No, but I'm hoping to be in a more active role than that. I'd rather be with a law firm than with a bank." Having had two or three of my classmates who didn't ever study, and didn't learn a thing, saying they didn't need to because they would have a job at the trust department at the bank when they got out, I decided that was not my best career move.

"The only other places I can think of," he said, "are maybe some of the big corporations. They have house counsel." I said, "Well, that would be more interesting to me than a bank. Do you have any in mind?" He finally said, after I just goaded him into naming one, "Well, Vulcan Materials has house counsel." I said, "Yes, I know that." I had heard that Barney Monaghan was the Vulcan Materials lawyer.

I told him that I'd heard good things about Mr. Monaghan. He said, "Maybe you ought to try there." He did not offer to call or otherwise introduce me, but he did suggest that I try there. I drove out to Vulcan Materials and asked to see Mr. Monaghan. Well, Mr. Monaghan was out of town.

I was passed off to an assistant who knew not much about anything and was distressed to be interviewing a woman. He kept exclaiming things like, "I'm shocked that Mr. Arant sent you. What was he doing? Lawyers here have to deal with lots of rough men, workers and truckers. You would be embarrassed. I can't imagine what he was thinking by sending you. Their language is highly unsuitable for a woman. He must be confused about our business."

I listened to him repeat variations of this silliness and finally in exhausted exasperation I said, "Are you trying to tell me that you think the old son-of-a-bitch is senile?"

JUST CALL ME JANIE

Janie, Dad, Verla

Janie and Verla

Janie's Maternal
Grandparents

Janie and Verla with Mom, Willie Scott Ledlow

Friend Daniel, Verla, Janie

Janie's Dad, John Ledlow

Janie's Family

Janie and Verla

Janie, Mom, Verla

Janie, Dad, Verla

Janie, High School Graduation

Just Call Me Janie

Section Two

Rights

Just Call Me Janie

JANIE SHORES

RIGHTS

"A STATE SUPREME COURT'S RESPONSIBILITY IS TO CORRECT ERRORS OF LOWER COURTS, DECIDING CASES BASED SOLELY ON U.S. LAW, REGARDLESS OF THE PERSONAL POLITICS AND PREFERENCES OF THE JUDGES."

USLEGAL.COM

CONTENTS

INTERVIEW IV – 12/05/2010: **FROM JANIE'S SUMMARIES TO THE SUPREME COURT**
PAGE 127

INTERVIEW V – 12/12/2010: **COFFEE WITH BEAR BRYANT; CAKE WITH MORRIS DEES**
PAGE 149

INTERVIEW VI – 1/11/2011: **A JUDGE'S WORK IS NEVER DONE**
PAGE 167

PHOTOS
PAGE 189

Just Call Me Janie

INTERVIEW IV

FROM JANIE'S SUMMARIES TO THE SUPREME COURT

Arden: Janie, what prompted you to run for Judge of the Alabama Supreme Court?
Janie: I'll tell you a little about what led up to it. When I graduated from law school in '59, and my mentor Vince Kilborn gave me the first job I ever had out of high school, he recommended me to Judge Simpson of the Supreme Court to be his law clerk. Fortunately, he'd already had one woman law clerk and found her to be very efficient and satisfactory. He called me and hired me, sight unseen.

Since I'd had trouble getting a job as a lawyer for a firm, I opened my own law office in Selma, where I was living. Of course, I didn't have much of a private practice. When I agreed to be Judge Simpson's law clerk, I asked if he had any objection to my doing the work in Selma, an hour's drive from Montgomery. He agreed. I clerked for him for a year, driving back and forth as required, resisting moving to Montgomery, the state capital. The usual law clerk term is one year, but at the end of that first year, he asked me to stay on for another year.

During that year, I had moved to Birmingham where I finally had gotten a job as an attorney with Liberty National. I was there when I got the call to help Judge Simpson again. He had been involved in an automobile accident and needed help with his cases. He called me because we had worked together very successfully from two locations when I lived in Selma. I was happy to help him and I had time to do so. I would pick up the record and the briefs, draft an opinion, and send it to him. He and his devoted, efficient secretary would handle the rest of it.

Arden: Would he consult with you on what the opinion was going to be, or did you draft it?

Janie: I had access to the record of the case and the briefs. Most of the time I'd use my own judgment and draft the opinion based upon the facts and the law. He seldom told me how to decide a case. I never found that he had any objective other than to get it right legally. Sometimes I felt that it would be helpful to me to hear the oral arguments. At such a time, I would have his secretary send me a transcript of the oral arguments and I would listen to that as well as read the record and briefs.

Many times I found it necessary to satisfy myself that I was getting it right, to do further research, beyond what the briefs included. Of course, sometimes he would say what his impression about the outcome should be based upon the arguments and what his inclinations were with respect to a case.

The Case for Retirement

At that time, in Alabama, most of the appellate judges and all of the Supreme Court justices were underpaid and the retirement benefits were inadequate. There was almost no administrative help provided to the appellate courts. Many of the judges were past retirement age and tired of working but because of the inadequacy of their retirement benefits, they had little choice but to stay on the courts.

The Chief Justice at the time was much revered and respected but he was exhausted by his many unsuccessful efforts to get the legislature to properly fund the judicial branch. Finally, he did retire, and a younger, energetic, much-admired lawyer named Howell Heflin ran for the office of Chief Justice. Heflin promised to amend the constitution of the state and completely rewrite the Judicial Article. The Alabama state constitution had been adopted originally in 1901. It had been amended many times. It is a famously outdated document, inadequate for contemporary issues.

Under the 1901 constitution, it was virtually impossible to address the 1970s and '80s needs of the courts. Nothing short of a constitutional amendment would do that; however, amending the constitution by re-writing the entire Judicial Article was an enormous political challenge. That reality accounted for the fact that the daunting task of updating it had not been undertaken earlier.

Legislative partial fixes were tried, such as the creation of inferior courts with limited but specific jurisdiction to address the needs of local communities. There was no uniformity among these courts, and each had its own rules of procedure.

Heflin promised to address the constitution problem by writing and undertaking to have adopted by statewide vote a new Judicial Article. He succeeded. That impressive success and the implementation efforts that followed gained national attention and admiration.

Among the provisions of the new Judicial Article was a mandatory retirement age for judges and, for the first time, a provision for the legislature to fund judicial retirement. This new provision led to an unusually high number of vacancies on the courts of the state when elderly judges quickly retired.

In 1972, I decided to run for one of those vacant seats on the Supreme Court. At this time, I had been teaching at Cumberland Law School since about 1966. I knew, therefore, quite a few former students who were now practicing young lawyers. These young lawyers lived in various locations throughout the state.

A sizable additional group of Alabama lawyers were familiar with my name from the fact that *Janie's Summaries* that I had written in my student days had become widely distributed among law students who attended college after me. In a court race that normally would not draw wide interest from anyone but lawyers, name recognition among lawyers is obviously very helpful.

A vacancy on the Supreme Court occurred when the incumbent Judge Goodwyn died after having qualified to run for re-election in the Democratic Primary. There was no Republican candidate. These events meant that the Executive Committee of the Democratic Party had the authority to name a candidate for the seat.

At this time, there were no Republican state office holders. Even at that late date, the Republican Party had not yet lived down its role in the Civil War and freeing the slaves. In response to that history, the South had become totally Democratic.

Today the situation is the opposite. There are no Democratic state office holders The Democrats have lost majority public favor for the same reason that the Republicans did earlier. The Democratic Party is identified with supporting the Voting Rights Act and all of the liberal social legislation of the 1960s. Racial struggles have dominated politics in Alabama more than a century.

Several lawyers called to encourage me to seek the nomination to the vacant seat on the Supreme Court. At that time, there were only 22 members of the Democratic Executive Committee. My long-time friend Bob Vance was Chairman. Later, he and George Wallace would compete for control of the Committee.

After I committed to seek the nomination, Jimmy Bloodworth, a respected Circuit Judge from Decatur, also announced that he was seeking the nomination. Jimmy and I were seeking the endorsements of those 22 Democratic Executive Committee members. I called on all of them and in the end I secured just one vote less than half. Jimmy got the nomination. I later served on the Court with Jimmy for several years.

That effort that occurred in 1968 or 1969 became useful experience when I ran for State Supreme Court in 1972. By '72, the Judicial Article had passed. It included a provision requiring the legislature to fund judicial retirement and also included an age restriction. This allowed a number of incumbent judges who had been willing but unable to retire to do so. Two vacancies came open on the state Supreme Court.

I qualified for one of those seats on the first day for qualifying established by the Democratic Executive Committee. No one else qualified until the last day of the qualifying period. I didn't really expect to have no opposition, but neither did I expect to have so much. On the last day when I called to see if I had any opposition, four other candidates had qualified for that seat.

One was Eric Embry, a good lawyer who had argued the *New York Times v. Sullivan* case before the Supreme Court of the United States. He was a member of a good Birmingham law firm. The founding member of that firm, Roderick Beddow had a national reputation as a criminal defense trial lawyer.

Also qualifying was Arthur Goldthwaite from a prestigious Montgomery law firm and a prominent family. His grandfather had been the Chief Justice of the Supreme Court. I thought both of them were formidable candidates in opposition. Both were known as good lawyers and both had broad contacts throughout the state.

Then a third candidate from Tuscaloosa had qualified and would be on the ballot as F.O. Fant. He was known and always referred to by his nickname, "Buckethead" Fant. I don't know why, but it didn't seem to be used derisively when I asked people who he was. Buckethead seemed to be a term of endearment.

The Faux Faulkner

Finally, a fourth candidate had qualified named James Faulkner. At the time, I didn't know a lawyer by that name, and neither did anybody else in town. It turned out that he was a little-known sole practitioner in Shelby County. He had been encouraged to run by an acquaintance who thought he might have a chance because people would confuse him with another well-known Jimmy Faulkner, the candidate I had worked for in the 1958 governor's race.

The "real" Jimmy Faulkner was a well-respected Baldwin County newspaper publisher who had become an active supporter of Governor George Wallace. The real Jimmy Faulkner had name recognition that exceeded all of the other candidates for the Supreme Court. The little-known Faulkner Faulkner was not a lawyer. For his candidacy, although he had never been called "Jimmy" in his adult life, he took to referring to himself as Jimmy Faulkner to confuse voters.

On top of that, faking innocence, he told people that I was married to Arthur Shores, a black lawyer. In the run-off election between faux Faulkner and me, he elaborated on this theme and passed out campaign literature (usually in the form of flyers placed on windshields in big-city parking lots) saying that his white female opponent was married to Arthur Shores. Arthur Shores was well known. Not only was he among the first black lawyers to be admitted to the bar in Alabama, he was frequently in the news because his house was all too frequently targeted and bombed by the KKK and their sympathizers.

Arden: So it was you and James Faulkner who became the top two out of the five candidates for the state Supreme Court?

Janie: Yes, and the experienced candidates, the ones I thought would be hard for me to beat, Eric Embry and Goldwaithe, didn't do nearly as well.

Realizing that his good showing was based upon people confusing him with the prominent Jimmy Faulkner the newspaper publisher, my opponent did all he could to compound the confusion. I did what little I could to convince voters that my opponent was not who he claimed to be and that I was not who he said I was, but it would have taken a lot more resources than I had to have been successful at that.

My political problems were confounded by the fact that in the run-off election there were only two statewide races on the ballot: the Supreme Court race, between the wrong Faulkner and me; and Bull Connor, the racist police commissioner of Birmingham who was running for the Public Service Commission against somebody I forget. Bull's position on race was well known from the police dogs and fire hoses he used to break up marches. Faux Faulkner had been a member of the Sovereignty Commission, a racist group. It was a perfectly dreadful experience, and I lost.

The Admirable Judge Simpson

Arden: When you were clerking for Judge Simpson, I'm interested in whether there were any specially significant cases that you decided when he didn't provide you with much information, and you really wrote the opinion?

Janie: There were a lot of them, most of them actually. I read the record, studied the briefs and law, and applied the law. That is what a law clerk is supposed to do. That is all that Judge Simpson expected me to do. Never once did he attempt to direct the outcome of any case. He expected me to be totally objective about the legality of a case, and I tried to be.

I was happy to help Judge Simpson with the workload. There was nothing wrong with his mind. He never lost any of his intellectual power, which was immense. He continued to function fully. He attended oral arguments and court conferences. He presented his cases. Other members of the Court were very much aware of Judge Simpson's physical challenges after the car accident, but there was never a suggestion that he was unable to perform the functions of the office. All of the justices had law clerks who helped with the often staggering caseloads.

I admired Judge Simpson enormously; he was determined, as much as possible, to get every case right as far as the law was concerned. That was his charge to me, to get it right. I never knew him to cast a vote in a case or write one that deviated from that.

Arden: You sought the appointment to fill the court vacancy in 1968, but you ran in 1971. Three years went by in between. What occurred during those three years. Were you strategizing about running?

Janie: I realized that because of the advanced ages of the justices, there were bound to be some court vacancies coming up. A number of the judges were well over 70. The primary thing that happened in that interval was the passage of the first major revision of the state constitution since 1901.

Howell Heflin, himself Chief Justice by then, had worked to get the constitutional amendment relating to the judiciary passed. When it was adopted and for the first time provided for the retirement of judges with benefits, judges all over the state, not only Supreme Court judges but also circuit judges and all the judges who met the requirements, did retire.

The new Judicial Article created a whole new landscape with respect to the judiciary. It created a level of trial judges that we had never had before, and that also meant a whole raft of candidates would be running for those positions. So, it was not unanticipated that there would be vacancies throughout the system if the Judicial Article passed. Along with many others, I anticipated running again when the time was right.

Arden: In the vote in which James Faulkner and you were the two people in the run-off, how do you account for the run-off vote? He got votes because of his fake name; but Eric Embry and Goldwaite were well-known attorneys while you weren't as well known. Yet you were the person who ended up in the run-off.

Janie: I think one key factor went back to my law school days. I wrote those summaries and shared them freely, and a lot of people benefited from that. Many of my classmates and many who came after me benefited from the summaries and always acknowledged it, and thanked me for it. By the time I ran, those people had been practicing all over the state for close to 20 years. Most of them had become respected members of their communities and they remembered me, not only because we had been classmates but also because they had benefited from *Janie's Summaries*. That process created a base of support for me that none of my fellow candidates had.

Colleagues would frequently introduce me at political gatherings in their communities during the campaign and almost without exception emphasized their opinion that "she was the smartest one in our class." That might not count for much in a legislative race (or governor's, as history shows) but I think that people do want judges to be smart.

I also had another advantage in a statewide race. I had nine years' worth of graduates of Cumberland Law School located throughout the state. As it turned out, I knew, or was known to, at least one lawyer in almost every county in the state, and that was a real advantage. On the other hand, Eric knew or was known to all the lawyers in the city of Birmingham.

Arden: But not throughout the state.

Janie: I had the positive name recognition advantage running in a statewide race. It made the difference, unquestionably.

Sex & the Supreme Court

Arden: Your reputation and your persona, obviously influenced a lot of the people including your classmates and students and others. Do you think your sex had anything at all to do with some people voting for you?

Janie: Or against me? I would think so. I can't prove this scientifically, but I would imagine, based upon the experience I later had on the bench with sexism, that to the older lawyers it would have been a factor.

Sometimes an older lawyer who had been there many times before would be presenting an oral argument in an important case. He was no longer awed by being there. He was interested in presenting his case. Not infrequently, he would address the Court, "Your Honors and Mrs. Shores."

Arden: Not deliberately trying to be demeaning?

Janie: No. And it happened more than once. It was always the older, accomplished lawyers, the ones who were experienced and no longer had to mentally prepare for the formalities of the argument. Once, one of the older, experienced lawyers asked me what he should call me, as though he couldn't fathom calling a woman, "Your Honor."

Arden: As if to say, "There's something wrong about this picture." Did you ever acknowledge that he had singled you out?

Janie: Only once did I make him apologize, and that's because it wasn't his first time to do it. I asked him if he meant to imply that I was less honorable, or what.

Arden: Do you remember what he said?

Janie: He didn't say anything; he went on with his argument. It was almost an unconscious remark of his anyway. That's a phrase that you say when you're preparing to start your argument. It's like addressing an audience before a speech by saying "ladies and gentlemen;" it is purely impersonal, reflexive. Once I told him that he could "just call me Janie" if he was in such distress over using my actual title.

Her First Campaign

Arden: In that first campaign, did you travel the state?

Janie: There are sixty-seven counties and there are more than sixty-seven courthouses. I traveled to every courthouse. Judicial campaigns back then required the candidate to show up. There was no television advertising. I didn't have any experts running polls or consulting. I depended on word of mouth recommendations from lawyers and judges.

I spent a total of $34,000 on that first race. Sometimes a local lawyer would get the local radio station in a town to run an ad endorsing one or another of the judicial candidates, but there was virtually no television advertising.

Arden: Do you remember how significant your 1971 election loss was?

Janie: Not much. It was a very close race.

Arden: What did you decide to do next?

Janie: I ran again two years later when there was another vacancy created by the retirement of yet another member of the Court whose term was up and he was eligible to retire.

Arden: When you lost was there a question in your mind that you were prepared to run again?

Janie: No. I ran and in '74. I was elected and took office in January of '75. I had only one opponent that time, a Circuit Judge from somewhere in the southeastern part of the state. I won handily that time.

Arden: Did you spend a large part of those two years campaigning?

Janie: Not really, because in a judicial race traditionally there's no campaigning to be done. The main thrust is on going to see the lawyers, as many as you can, and hopefully in groups because they are key to your election and getting as many endorsements as you can. That's about it, particularly in my case, in which there were no other statewide races.

Arden: How was your reception by the Court and the bar?

Janie: There had been pretty much a transformation of the members of the court during those six years. First, Jimmy Bloodworth won when it was up to the Democratic Party, that was '68 or '69, and Faulkner won in '72. There was another vacancy that year, and Red Jones won.

When I finally ran, there were two more vacant seats. Eric Embry got elected to one of those positions. Reneau Almon got elected to another. Almon was on the Court of Criminal Appeals, having been appointed by Governor Albert Brewer. He was a sitting judge on the Court of Criminal Appeals. The three of us took the oath on the same day. We were sworn in by Howell Heflin, the author of the constitutional amendment that had made the positions available.

The Seniority Factor

I remember asking my friend, John David Snodgrass, who was a Circuit Court judge in Huntsville and a classmate of mine, "What possible difference can seniority make?" Previously, Reneau Almon had come to me to discuss seniority. He said that we should decide the seniority question since we were about to be sworn in. I told him I would think about it and immediately called John David.

I said to him, "What possible difference can seniority make?" Turns out it does make a real difference. You are assigned office space based on seniority. You are assigned cars based on seniority. Much significant procedure is determined by seniority.

I got together with Reneau and we made an agreement. I told him, "You can be senior of the three of us coming on because you've already served on the Court of Criminal Appeals for six or seven years. I'll be next after that, because I've been around here a long time. Eric can be third."

Arden: What did Eric have to say about that?

Janie: Nothing.

Arden: Was Howell Heflin still Chief Justice? What was that day like?

Janie: I do have lots of pictures of that, by the way. It was a lot of press because somebody told me, I have never known if it was true or not, but I was later told I was the first woman appellate judge to be elected in America. So we did have lots of national media. There were two other women I knew of who were on appellate courts, but they'd been appointed by the governor. Susie Sharp in South Carolina was one of them.

Arden: You were the first U.S. State Supreme Court woman judge elected?

Janie: I know I was among the first women, if not the first. The swearing in was a memorable occasion. A large contingent of the black community was there, for which I was most grateful. There are photos of Dr. Gaston and his wife Minnie. Chris McNair, whose daughter was killed in that church bombing, took the pictures. I think because of the liberal balance and the constitutional amendment and a woman breaking the white male barrier, the day marked a kind of hopeful breakthrough for blacks too.

Oscar Adams, the first black ever to be elected in Alabama, would be elected to the Supreme Court a few years later. I served on the court with him until he retired. Also because there were three judges being sworn in at once, there were heaps of families, supporters, and friends.

Arden: What day of the week was that?

Janie: It always takes place on a Monday.

Arden: Then you set out to work. What was that like?

Janie: As on the Supreme Court of the United States, the work takes place in offices and chambers other than the actual Supreme Court, but the oral arguments are there. The official chambers is the setting that the public sees. I don't remember the first case we heard *en banc*, but I do remember ones of real interest in which the courtroom was full of spectators, which was usually the case in any event.

I hired a law clerk and settled into my office. The month is divided up into the oral argument week, and then there's the conference week when we meet, vote and consider cases, and so on.

The Court sits in two divisions named after the senior-most member of each division. In our case, one of the reasons for my wanting to be senior to Eric was so that I could sit on the panel with Judge Merrill, who was then the oldest one left. He was a contemporary of Judge Simpson. I'd known him many years and admired him greatly.

There was the Merrill division and there was the Bloodworth division. Bloodworth had been elected back when the Committee was doing the choosing, and he had advanced enough to become the head of a division. There was a rapid turnover in a very few years. The rapid turnover was because he was already head of one of the divisions.

I could have been the head of a division, although I never did. The Chief Justice sits on both divisions. Divisions are known by the senior-most judges. They alternate by seniority.

Arden: How many judges in each division?

Janie: Five including the Chief Justice.

Selecting Cases

Arden: What's the process for selection of cases that are accepted for argument in the Supreme Court of Alabama?

Janie: It's unlike in the Supreme Court of the United States, in which all cases, once accepted, are orally argued. Cases usually get to the Supreme Court of the United States on a petition for *certiorari*, which is either granted or denied.

The Supreme Court of Alabama hears appeals as a matter of right from the Court of Criminal Appeals and the Court of Civil Appeals, both of which were created because of the vast number of appeals from the Circuit Courts, which are again a matter of right.

Arden: Did that occur because of the new Judicial Article?

Janie: No, that's always been the case. The Court of Criminal Appeals and the Court of Civil Appeals were created quite a number of years ago to handle the increasing caseloads of appeals from the trial courts in Alabama, called the Circuit Courts. A party who loses a case in the trial court, that is the

Circuit Court, can appeal as a matter of right. This created an unbearable burden on the Supreme Court.

In an effort to lessen the overload, the legislature created two courts of lesser jurisdiction: a Court of Civil Appeals and a Court of Criminal Appeals. From those two courts, the Supreme Court reviews issues on petitions for *certiorari*. On the criminal side, if it's a death penalty case, it's a matter of right.

Arden: Tell me about the relationships you had with the judges when you entered.

Janie: I generally had a very good relationship. First of all, I was familiar with the procedures, having been there for so long as a clerk and having worked closely with Judge Simpson. I knew the process as well as anyone there.

Except for the oral arguments and the case conferences in which we vote on cases, day to day, you're mostly working in your own office with your own staff. There's not much ongoing interchange among judges. I didn't see many of them until I got to the case conferences.

A Birmingham Tradition Begins

Since I stayed in Birmingham and didn't move to Montgomery to maintain a permanent office, that lack of social interchange was especially true. Red Jones and Eric Embry didn't move to Montgomery either. I established a pattern that persists to this day. Some still don't move to Montgomery. You might argue that's not a good thing; I would argue that it is a good thing because I found that Montgomery has but one subject -- state politics -- and it permeates everything and that can be stifling.

It was refreshing, I think, certainly to Howell Heflin, for some of us to come in for conference, and we hadn't heard a bumbling word about whatever was the gossip or worry in Montgomery. We'd been way off in Birmingham

The dean of Cumberland Law School where I had taught, Arthur Weeks, when I lost the '72 race, told me if I wanted to keep an office at the law school, he'd make space available to me and a law clerk. At the time, I was still in Birmingham anyway. Red Jones kept an office at Cumberland for years. Then when I came on the Court, I kept an office there with one of my law clerks who was located there. I only went to Montgomery for conferences or oral argument.

I kept a secretary and law clerk in Montgomery as well, for any emergency that came up; and that happened all the time, emergency appeals, something that has to be voted on, and so on. You need some staff in Montgomery to be efficient, but ninety-nine percent of my work took place in my Birmingham office.

Arden: How often would you go to Montgomery?

Janie: I went to Montgomery at least one day a week, depending on what the function was, and often three or four times a week. Sometimes I'd stay overnight. I tried that for a while, and decided that it was a bigger waste of time than driving back. The law clerks did the driving, and I could work on the way. I'd be home in the same time it would take to settle into a motel and all that. I finally made it a condition when I hired a law clerk that one of the responsibilities was to drive me to Montgomery, as required. For nine a.m. conferences, or nine o'clock oral arguments, we'd leave at seven a.m. and get there in plenty of time, often before the ones from Montgomery got there.

A Clerk on the Clock

Arden: Were there law clerks already assigned to you, or did you have a process of finding one? Who was your first law clerk?

Janie: They're not assigned; every judge hires his own law clerks without participation of anybody else. You hire whomever you want to be your law clerk. My first two law clerks were recent Cumberland students whom I had taught. I knew something about their abilities. Doug Ghee was one, and Rick Lyerly was the other.

Essentially, I tried to alternate between the schools, not always to have them from one place. As the years passed, I branched out and got some clerks from up East. Every once in a while, you'd find a Yankee soul that wanted to come South for the experience.

Arden: On that first day at the court, were applications from clerks waiting for you?

Janie: Not on the first day, but they would accumulate; you would get plenty of applications, lots and lots of them. There was no problem whatever to solicit applications; the problem was eliminating them down to whom you wanted. For one year, you are just living with them. There were two authorized when I got there. One clerk was not enough to handle the work volume we had. Now most of the justices have a staff attorney that just stays on plus one or two law clerks.

Arden: A law clerk term is two years, the last of which overlaps with the incoming clerk's first to provide some training and consistency.

Janie: I found that a one-year term was too short. By the time you get one trained to do the work the way that you want it done, the year's half over, and you've got to start from scratch with a new one.

Nobody Said It Was Easy

Arden: How long did it take for you to get up and running?

Janie: Not long. I was always chastised, and probably in truth, for not using my law clerks nearly as much as some of the others did. I wanted to make sure the opinion said what I wanted to say, so I did most of the writing myself. I would often write what I wanted to say and what I believed the law to be and then send the clerk off to look up some law that says this.

Arden: Did that habit stay with you throughout?

Janie: Pretty much. My name would be on that statement recorded in those books from now on. I wanted to know that I was confident of my opinion.

Arden: I understand the sentiment, but a lot of judges don't do that.

Janie: That's right. I'm not there, so I can't say for sure, but I don't think that I ever, in all the 24 years that I served, put out more than three decisions with no opinion. You know, affirmed, but no opinion attached to explain how I reached it.

Some of the justices left off opinions quite often. It did not indicate that the case was not carefully considered. To the contrary, we'd all been through it, battled it out and we all agreed that the trial judge got it right; so we took the position, let's affirm him and quit arguing about how we're going to do it, or vice versa.

On the other hand, a case is never reversed without an opinion. An appellate court owes the trial bench an explanation when it reverses a case; it can reverse only for error at trial.

The Alabama Supreme Court is now made up of different judges with different views. I notice that they have a very,

very limited number of cases that are argued orally. When I went on the court, all of the cases were orally argued. If either party asked for oral argument, it was granted. It was not uncommon to have a full week's worth of cases that were orally argued, usually hearing six cases a day. Nowadays it's rare that they will grant an oral argument. The present court issues far more memorandum opinions than we did. Those are orders with no written opinions at all; they are simply confirmed or reversed.

Arden: To what do you attribute that lack of written support?

Janie: I attribute it to volume, in one respect, to be charitable, but also to not demanding enough of the staff. It would take me as much time studying the case to decide that it could be affirmed without an opinion as it would to write an opinion. The process is exactly the same — but one version includes a document expressing the legal justification.

It concerns me greatly when I see a great percentage of decisions coming out with no opinion. You're sitting there trying to vote right and what I would have done, if it were me, I would not always have read the record in a case assigned to another judge. You just can't read all the records, but I would have read the brief on both sides of the legal argument. I also would have formed some preliminary opinion on how I think it ought to go, based on my recollection of what the law is, what the briefs tell me the law is, and so on. I'd develop a pretty firm opinion as to whether I would vote to affirm or reverse.

It is encouraging to read an opinion that goes through the process of establishing how the author of it got to that conclusion. Very comforting. I have a few times changed my mind from my preliminary reaction, and that was the way I'd do it. I'd always read the briefs first before I'd read the proposed opinion. I'd form my own impression of the legal issue before I'd pick up the proposed opinion. If it came out differently from what my reaction had been, then I'd be really careful about the way I read it. This kind of research is time consuming, but it gives me some comfort that the vote I cast was right, that it expressed my opinion. I'm afraid that process has been weakened somewhat now.

Arden: Perhaps the judges themselves don't accept discipline.

Janie: It can become too easy to trust one another's opinions; or it can become easy to form an idea of what result you'd like to reach. But it's harder to get to a considered legal conclusion following the logic of the law about the particular issue step, by step, by step.

Arden: And it's more time consuming.

Janie: Yes, definitely more time consuming. Always you can rationalize, "Well, it's not going to do anything to change the law. It won't add one word to the literature. Too bad for these parties if the decision comes out wrong, but it won't hurt the body of the law."

The lack of researched and considered legal verifications for a decision leads to practices that can jeopardize the rights of the people involved in the case; and I think that it's a violation of the judicial oath that you take; you swear to base your decisions on established laws. The job holds a great responsibility. You know, nobody said it was easy.

Just Call Me Janie

Interview V

Coffee with Bear Bryant; Cake with Morris Dees

Arden: Did you keep in touch and remain friends with Vince Kilborn during those years?

Janie: Yes. Of course, I was gone from the Mobile area for a long time but I did stay in touch with him and his wife Mary Jo, Sonny's mother. I was often invited to visit during Mardi Gras and remember once when I was in law school coming to attend the Crew of Columbus ball.

His son, Vincent III, who was called Sonny as a boy and is still Sonny to me, lives right down the bay from me. I see quite a lot of him. He is very attentive to me and includes me in social gatherings, which he has frequently.

He has a very successful law practice and seems determined to make a significant contribution to cancer research. He also supports underprivileged and impaired children, not just financially but with his presence. He has established an organization called Kilborn Kids through which he supports them.

Recently he gave a sizable financial contribution to the cancer center at the University of South Alabama. He has a natural interest in cancer research because so many of his male relatives have been victims of it. His father was the oldest of four brothers: Vince, Charlie, John, and Ben. Ben, the youngest one, lived the longest and died at 54. All the others died before they were 54.

The oldest Vince died from pancreatic cancer in the early 1970s. He was still alive in 1968 when I was being considered for an appointment to the Court, but then when I ran in 1972, he was no longer living. His brother Charlie had died of a heart attack some years before then. Then the others died.

Kilborn Connections

Arden: How long did you work for Mr. Kilborn?

Janie: Four years. We gradually became friends and he and Mary Jo visited me in Selma at least twice, I recall. And we kept up with each other.

Arden: He mentored you to pursue your legal education to become something other than a secretary.

Janie: He said he thought that I had an inherent ability to understand the law that he found unusual in somebody as young as I was at 17 or 18 years old.

Arden: What kind of events prompted remarks like that?

Janie: When I first started work with his firm, he dictated everything. Later on we got a Dictaphone, but mostly in the years I was there I used shorthand. He dictated letters, deeds, contracts, pleadings, everything. Mobile was unusual in that the old common law system of pleading at length was still used. If one mastered that complex system, it provided an understanding of the law that was useful in every area of the law and especially so in the study of law.

Arden: Meaning you pled everything.

Janie: Yes. Alabama had not legislatively adopted any system of "code" pleading. It had not adopted a form of pleading based upon the Federal Rules of Procedure. It would do so in the 1960s, but Mobile continued to "plead at length" for a long time, even after the legislature acted. In Mobile, a real distinction, a literal distinction, between law and equity was maintained for a long time after code pleading was adopted.

During one of those long sessions of dictation, Mr. Kilborn was making some point or argument and I, uncharacteristically, commented on the substance of the argument. I said something like, that wouldn't work. If that were true we couldn't have life estates in real estate, or some similar observation.

I don't remember now the context in which he was making the point but I was listening to the substance of the point he was making, which I didn't always do. It is not necessary to follow the substance of dictation to be able to reproduce accurately what is dictated. But this time I must have been following the point he was making to have interjected a critique of it.

I interposed a comment about a subject of which I knew nothing and compared it to one of which I knew even less. But that kind of thing caused him to comment more than once that I had a good mind for the law.

Arden: Was he happy to see you go to school?

Janie: Delighted that I went to law school. Absolutely delighted, and kept up with my progress.

Miss Rosa Gerhardt

In the 1960s and '70s, it was not usual for women to be in law school. I knew of only one woman lawyer in Mobile in the years I was there, but she was working as a secretary. Her name was Miss Rosa Gerhardt. I don't think she ever practiced law. Years later, Judge Dan Thomas, a U.S. District judge, hired her in some quasi-legal capacity.

I was gone quite a long time from the area in which I grew up, but I returned frequently. My parents still lived in the same town, and I visited fairly regularly. I bought the first house I owned in Montrose here in 1972. My husband and I continued to live in Birmingham, but spent a lot of time in what we called our summerhouse. While we considered Birmingham our principal residence, we maintained a presence in the Mobile-Baldwin County area all these years.

Being gone most of the time, even if you return for short periods, you lose contact with people. My life-long friends from school days are limited to two or three who were classmates from the very beginning. I saw a couple of them not too long ago. I had lunch with two of the girls and one boy. He fetched us all and drove us down to Gulf Shores for our high school reunion.

School Ties that Bind

One old friend went to Auburn for college and remained there after graduation. He has been very successful, having started off building student housing at Auburn, and stayed there in real estate development in and around the university.

Another was Mary Jean Dean. She married Gordon Barnhill and still lives on the property his family owned and farmed when we were children. I asked her recently whether she agreed with me that our parents and teachers never talked to us about college. She said they did not, but that she would not have listened to them if they had because she had already decided to marry Gordon by the time the subject would have come up.

She got into real estate sales and she said she has made a living selling the same property over and over. She was referring to the fact that real estate development and increasing population in the county has seen farm after farm divided into subdivisions all over the county.

Competition with Max

Many of the pals I had in law school have remained life-long friends. In my own class was Max Rogers. His formal full name is imposing: Charles McPherson Augustin Rogers, III. His father was a member of a prominent old Mobile law firm, McCorvey, Turner, Rogers, Johnstone, and Adams. Max went to Williams College, a venerable old private boys' school located in Massachusetts. It finally started admitting women in about 1970.

Max came back to the University of Alabama for law school. He and I were always competing for number one in the class in terms of grade performance. Both of us made excellent grades. Some semesters he would beat me; sometimes I would beat him.

Because we consistently led the class, we were thrown together a lot. The first in the class automatically is elected editor-in-chief of the law review. The second in academic performance becomes associate editor. The top four students academically constitute the moot court team, editor of the law review, and associate editors. The whole board of the law review is assigned on the basis of grade point average by virtue of performance. Because of this, Max and I spent a lot of time together and became good friends. We were moot court partners and researched the law and wrote the briefs and argued the case before a panel of Supreme Court justices. We won, too.

We were so close in academic standing that it was necessary to check at the end of every semester to see who was first in the class. Because of this, it was apparent that we were going to be competing for editor-in-chief of the law review. Right up to the last moment.

Law Review

At one point, the subject came up and I acquiesced or might have suggested that since I wasn't likely to be recruited for a leading law firm, that it would mean more to his career to be the editor of the law review than for me to be it. Max was very likely to be recruited, but he would no doubt return to his father's major law firm in Mobile in any event.

Arden: Do you mean that because sex discrimination would probably block your chances in any hiring situation, the position on your resume wouldn't have made as much difference to you?

Janie: That's right. It wouldn't have improved my odds of being hired enough to count; so he became editor of the law review and I became associate editor. We continued to be paired the last year we were in law school together.

One of the advantages of being editors of the law review was that we got office space and access to the building. We could come and go at any hour. Both of us were morning people, so we were often in our offices in the law review section of the building early in the morning. From that vantage point, we saw Coach Bryant almost every morning.

It was Coach Bryant's practice to go to Druid Drug Store, located just east of the law school, for morning coffee. As I mentioned, Max had gone to undergraduate school at Williams College up East and therefore had no exposure to a real football program. After several embarrassing years under Coach (Ears) Whitworth, the University had persuaded Paul (Bear) Bryant to come back to his alma mater as coach.

Coffee with Bear Bryant

Max and I developed a practice of also going to Druid Drug Store for coffee at the same time Coach Bryant went. It is a small drug store, it was early morning and often Coach Bryant, Max and I were the only customers. After a time, he began to join us if we got there first, or invite us to join him if somehow he had managed to get there without our seeing him. He never told us any team secrets, but he was cordial, entertaining, and often curious about what we did reviewing law all the time.

Max was a slight, somewhat fragile person, not an athletic prospect at all. But he loved Coach Bryant and those early morning coffee sessions. And I did, too. We'd had a dismal football performance the whole time I'd been at Alabama. It was so bad that the usual thing that you'd see on Monday morning when I was in undergraduate school was Coach Whitworth (we called him Ears Whitworth) hanged in effigy in front of the student union building. So a new coach of any kind was welcomed to the University of Alabama with genuine glee. That new coach turned out to be the impressive Coach Bryant.

Many years later, after what must have been an Alabama-Auburn football game in Birmingham, Bob and Helen Vance and Jim and I were sitting in The Club after the ballgame. I don't remember the game or the score, but we must have won because I do remember that we were seriously celebrating.

In came Coach Bryant and Mr. Lackey, either Julian or Rufus. They are brothers and both were good friends of Coach Bryant. I knew one of them. He served on the Board of Directors of Liberty National, and I saw him at board meetings. When she saw them, Helen said, "Oh, I would love to meet Coach Bryant." I responded, "Well, I know him. I'll introduce you."

We casually wandered out onto the patio behind them. They could not get back into the club without passing us, and as they turned and approached us, I spoke to them and said, "I would like for you to meet my friend Helen Vance." They both were very gracious to her and gracious to me, expressing how happy they were to meet Helen and how nice to see me again. As they walked away, I heard Mr. Lackey ask Coach Bryant about me: "Who is that little lady? I know her face but I can't think of her name." Coach Bryant responded, "I can't either, but she used to work at Druid Drug Store."

I came to believe that men see women differently than they see other men (no innuendo intended). It's an interesting fact.

The Invisible Woman

The first time I ran for the Supreme Court, I felt comfortable at the prospect of campaigning in Mobile. Every candidate for a judgeship knows that lawyers are the voters most interested in those judicial races. By virtue of having spent four years as a legal secretary, I knew most of the lawyers in Mobile.

I soon learned that while I knew them, they did not know me. I came to understand that secretaries, for the most part, make no impression on lawyers having business with the firm. They had no recollection of me. Neither my face nor my name prompted any recollection of having known me at all. Most were gracious enough and interested enough, and almost all were astonished, incredulous even, to hear that I was running for the Court but they had no ability to connect either my name or my face with those prior years.

I came to believe that for the most part, women in the workplace made no impression on men having business there. They were just part of the setting, like a part of the fixtures. Now I don't mean to suggest that a particularly spectacular looking secretary would have gone un-noted, but as a general rule, the women on the staff were simply not noticed.

Arden: Not persons.

Janie: Yes, part of the equipment and furniture. Which I just found perplexing.

Arden: You worked there for four years and met all these people and they didn't even remember where?

Janie: It's still interesting to me. The lack of curiosity, if nothing else, is interesting.

I thought of Bryant's response over the years. "I'm not sure what her name is, but she used to work at Druid Drug Store." Coach Bryant at least remembered *where* he had seen me. The lawyers didn't remember even that.

I am convinced that much of that has changed now. It is probably still common to see an all-female lower-post staff in law firms, but by now most, certainly all, the big firms also have a significant number of women lawyers.

Law School Friends

Arden: Who else did you run across in your law school while you were there?

Janie: Don Patterson was a friend. He became a circuit judge in Florence; Ben Reeves was a district attorney for many years.

Max Rogers practiced with his father's old firm for a long time and then became president of a bank.

Richard Shelby, who did not graduate from Alabama, but did get a law degree from Birmingham School of Law, was elected to the United States Senate. First, he was a Democrat, then switched to the Republican Party as whites in the South fled the Democratic Party, following the passage of the Civil Rights legislation in the 1960s. He has been re-elected ever since as a Republican and is still there.

John David Snodgrass remains a friend. I speak with him frequently. He served as a circuit judge in Huntsville for many years. He has now retired and returned to his beautiful farm on the Tennessee River in Scottsboro where he was born and raised. He was a year or so behind me in law school.

His girlfriend Annette Clark, one of the four other women in law school during my time, and I became friends and for a semester or so shared an apartment in Tuscaloosa. I was a year ahead of her in law school, but we got an apartment together and roomed together so I saw John David a lot because of Annette.

John David remains one of my closest friends. I suggested that he join me, Reneau Almon and his wife Debbie, and John T. Crowder and his wife Karen on a trip to Africa last year. It was a nice trip. John T. and Reneau were big-game hunters and have been on safari hunts many times. Each has an impressive collection of trophies. This time they were lion hunting. John David was not interested in joining them on the hunts, so he joined the women. He made friends everywhere we went. The staff at the hotel in Cape Town almost cried when he left a few days before the rest of us to return home.

Arden: Did he marry Annette Clark?

Janie: No, he did not. He never did get over it in my judgment, but she married a boy from Mississippi whom she met through me. She remained a friend until she died, and John David and I remain good friends to this day.

John David Snodgrass and Annette Clark are among the closest law school friends that I stayed in touch with forever. She later had married Hube Dodd, originally from Mississippi. She met him when he was at Craig Air Force Base in Selma. He was in the insurance business. They lived in Memphis for a long time and then came back to Birmingham. I was able to get her employed as the law librarian at Cumberland Law School since I was then teaching there. She later taught some courses and became very popular with the students.

Arden: Another testimony that women with law degrees can do anything.

Janie: That's right, if they're willing to do so. Dean Weeks, to his credit, bragged he was the first to recruit women professors.

After law school, John David went back to north Alabama where his roots truly are. His father had been a circuit judge. John David became a circuit judge in Huntsville. His father had founded a little bank in Scottsboro that later merged and became part of a bigger bank in Decatur, Alabama, the State National of Decatur. It was acquired later on by a bank in Birmingham founded and operated by Harry Brock, a very talented businessman.

John David, like his father, served on the board of directors of these banks, which through mergers and acquisitions have grown into an international financial institution.

John David, like his father and his maternal uncle Bob Jones, is a loyal Democrat. He is also loyal to his family traditions. I am sure he continues to run the farm just as his father did.

I doubt that he has ever sold a single acre of land, but I am sure he has bought some to add to the farm. I am equally sure that he hasn't sold any bank stock. He still buys a bunch of those cows every year, plants the pastures, and feeds the cows. They have calves and then you sell off the calves and then you do it all over again. One can understand why he loves his farm. It is a beautiful spot on Earth. The house sits on a mountain in overlooking the Tennessee River.

Morris & Millard Make History

Arden: You also were acquainted with Morris Dees.
Janie: Morris Dees and Millard Fuller. They were not in my class; I think they may have been a class behind me. I knew them fondly. They were talented entrepreneurs.

I was very impressed with their imagination. Their first venture that I knew anything about was supplying birthday cakes to students. That was an idea that Morris had. The whole project was accomplished within a week's time. Later, in their cookbook project. they wrote to every famous person they could think of asking for their favorite recipes, among them Jackie Kennedy, and published *The Famous People Recipes*, or some similar title. They applied the same technique to some project involving Christmas decorations that put buyer and seller together. Isn't that enterprising?

They were very successful. I don't know if this is true or not, but the story was that Millard told Morris that once they'd made a million dollars, he was going to quit SPLC and become a missionary and he did exactly that. Later on, he started Habitat for Humanity.

Aren't those wonderful life stories? Millard founded Habitat, and Morris was a founder of the successful Southern Poverty Law Center that has done some really good work. It makes one believe that there is a plan for all of us.

Limited Opportunities for Women in Law

Arden: Let's talk about what it was like being a woman who had her own law office in 1970s Alabama.

Janie: There were only a very few women lawyers then in Alabama. My guess is fewer than twenty. I only knew one other who had an office of her own. That was Miss Nina Miglionico from Birmingham.

Someone, it might have been Nina, suggested that we form a women's lawyers group, and we did. We met probably once a year. A male classmate running for some office in the state bar told me that if I could get the women lawyers to support him, then he would put one of us on a committee. I thought we instead should have tried to elect one or more of us to positions in the regular Alabama State Bar.

Women were just not seen as candidates for powerful jobs then. Even later, it was much the same. For instance, Sandra Day O'Connor in 1981 was appointed to the U.S. Supreme Court by President Ronald Reagan. She told a story about how her male law school classmates often remarked what a wonderful legal secretary she would make.

Arden: Did you get many customers?

Janie: I didn't get a staggering number of quality clients, but I got a lot of calls from loan companies inquiring whether I would handle collections for them. Automobile dealerships that carried their own paper called on me to determine whether I would do collections for them. A law license will get one all the work you want if you want to do collection work. That was certainly the case back then, and I doubt that it has changed much.

There was also plenty of opportunity in the domestic relations field. Many women, and some men, came to me to represent them in divorce or child custody matters. Those fields didn't interest me much, but I would agree to represent one of the parties in those cases from time to time, especially if it were referred to me by a friend, someone wanting to support my effort to succeed in Selma. Members of the Jewish community were especially thoughtful in this regard.

One of them recommended me to a woman who had moved to Selma. She was Mrs. Anthony J. Drexel, III. She had been married to Anthony Drexel of the Philadelphia Drexels, a prominent family.

Arden: There's a Drexel College.

Janie: Quite wealthy people. Anthony had died young and left a widow and at least two children who were then minors. Mrs. Drexel had been appointed by a Pennsylvania Court as the guardian of those children. She was required by that court order to file periodic reports on the guardianship estate. Now that she and the children were in Alabama and the children were still minors, she wanted the guardianship estate administered in Alabama, and retained me to represent her as guardian of those children. An annual accounting and a court order were required for expenditures of significant sums of money.

I remember petitioning the probate judge in Dallas County, Alabama, for what seemed to us a huge sum of money to fund the debut of the daughters. The judge was asked to approve that amount for that purpose. He and I agreed that he should appoint a guardian *ad litem* to represent the other side. We had a hearing, and the judge approved the amount requested. All of us thought the amount was perhaps more than a debut would cost in Selma, Alabama; however, there was no evidence that it was an unreasonable amount in Philadelphia.

Throughout the administration of this guardianship estate, I reported not only to Mrs. Drexel but also to the Drexel estate offices in Philadelphia. Mrs. Drexel and the children were delightful people.

Jewish Community in Selma

Mrs. Drexel was referred to me through mutual friends, Steve and Edie Ball. They had Rothschild's Dress Shop there where I shopped, and I often saw them.

There were several other Jewish families whom we saw with regularity. In fact, the Jewish community in Selma was prominent in civic leadership, and I think were totally welcomed and included in every civic endeavor. I don't recall any bias of any kind being expressed about them. This stands in sharp contrast to the attitude toward black people. I don't mean to imply that there was overt discrimination or criticism of the black people in early years when I was there, but it was there under the surface and soon became overt.

Arden: What about the bias against you because you were a woman?

Janie: Rarely was anything done or said overtly, but many conditions were in place that presented hurdles. For instance, the president of the Selma County Bar told me that I would be invited to join the bar association, but first the by-laws would have to be amended because membership then was limited to white male lawyers. He said he expected no opposition to an amendment allowing female white lawyers to admission. I've been asked whether I had more obstacles in my career due to my liberal politics or to my being a woman. Definitely the latter. Most judges on the court with me were liberal in their views about equal rights for blacks but not for women.

Of course, a black woman would have had double trouble. I had moved from Selma at the same time that the first black lawyer came to town. Hank and Rose Sanders, husband and wife, both lawyers, came not long after I moved. They soon were being noticed for being more assertive than the norm. They were expected to keep quiet about racism but they didn't. There was a voting rights drive that gained national attention in the early 1960s. Then came the Selma to Montgomery march.

Arden: Are there any more random thoughts you might have of those years prior?

Janie: No. The only thing that I should emphasize because it was truly important was the support I got when I was running for judge. I largely owe being elected to my law school classmates who used my notes. They really did feel an obligation to help me.

Keep in mind there hadn't been a Supreme Court race in years. There never had been in my colleagues' lifetimes, certainly. As I said, because there was no retirement for judges, they just stayed on until they died; then the governor would appointment somebody to take their place. And incumbents almost never had opposition. Because we were able to get a constitutional amendment that allowed for retirement, we had vacancies for the first time in years. An election for justices of the Supreme Court was as new to the trial lawyers as it was to us who were running.

Big Money, Less Justice, & Little Education

All these years I have been a proponent of letting the people elect the judges. I have argued that the voters have as much competence to elect an honest judge as they do to elect an honest governor. I should have learned something from observing how often that didn't work. I argued that we simply had to educate them in what to look for, that's all. But that's naive, that's really naive. No longer is it a free and open election. The decision to support or not support is made in boardrooms somewhere, anywhere in America, at the Chamber of Commerce. I am afraid money drives elections, and unfortunately that includes elections for judicial office.

Arden: The money does talk. No doubt about it. Wealthy businessmen read the electorate and they put the money where it best serves them.

Janie: That makes me sad because it will change the whole nature and the dynamic of the entire legal process. Karl

Rove came to Alabama in the nineties and set up shop in Montgomery to run the Supreme Court races and elected every Republican who was on the ballot that time.

Arden: Amazing.

Janie: I've traditionally defended the system of electing state judges. Some states have the so-called Missouri Plan and while I understand it takes the people out of the selection process, I have never been sure that it takes politics out of the process.

A committee of respected lawyers and perhaps non-lawyers sends a list to the governor, and he picks one from the list for appointment to a judgeship. It sounds good because in theory only qualified candidates get on the list from which the governor makes the selection. But we all know there is a difference between theory and practice.

Years ago, a similar plan for filling vacancies on the Birmingham bench existed. That committee sent three names to the governor for him to select from when a vacancy occurred. George Wallace was governor during one of his four terms, and he sent word back to the Birmingham committee that it could send names to him "all day long and all night long" but until Bill Jackson's name was on it, he was not going to select one. At least he was open about it.

Now that big money drives formerly non-partisan judicial races, just as it does all of the other political positions, I am losing my zeal for the popular election of judges. I don't have a better solution than our democratic one though.

I find myself coming back always to the same point. That is, the failure to educate people. I continue to believe that the greatest failure of our system is its failure to provide education and basic survival options to its people.

Arden: There's also a larger discrepancy in wealth now. Keeps getting larger.

Janie: It just boggles my mind that the wealth of the world is concentrated in the hands of a very small percentage of the population.

Arden: Exactly. It's sad.
Janie: And those same people want even more.

Just Call Me Janie

INTERVIEW VI

A JUDGE'S WORK IS NEVER DONE

Arden: Let's talk about the personalities from your Alabama Supreme Court years, how you were received, what your feelings were about being part of the Court, and more about specific cases and your impact on them.

Janie: It might be helpful to clarify that until Howell Heflin was elected as Chief Justice in 1970, the Alabama Constitution of 1901 had hampered progress in Alabama in many ways. It was a document designed to do just that. It remains an embarrassment.

An Embarrassment of Racists

Written in 1901 by a group of white racists not adjusted to losing the Civil War, it had one purpose in mind and that was to keep everything just like it was then. This old document has been amended hundreds of times. I think it's the longest state constitution in America, or close to being. Many efforts over the years have been undertaken to write a new constitution. Somehow no one seemed to be able to toss it out and start anew with an up to date one.

One of the most progressive governors we have had, at least in my lifetime, was Albert Brewer. He appointed yet another blue ribbon committee to write a constitution in the 1970s. This committee was chaired by Dean Leigh Harrison. Some of the brightest lawyers in the state worked on it, including me. We delivered the final draft to the governor, who presented it to the legislature, and we never heard another word about it. It is probably in a file or on a dusty shelf in Montgomery along with countless other efforts to improve Alabama's embarrassing 1901 constitution.

Howell Heflin, as the newly elected Chief Justice, concentrated on a new Judicial Article only. That first required passage by the legislature and then adoption by a vote of the people. It was on the ballot in a special election in December of 1972, I think.

As a supporter of the amendment, I spoke anywhere you could get a group to listen, asking voters to support the constitutional amendment. As I recall, the constitutional amendment was the only item on the ballot in that special election, and it passed by a narrow margin. Among other things, it gave the Supreme Court rulemaking authority, created a system of inferior courts, established an administrative agency to support the entire state judicial system, and finally provided for a retirement system for all judges.

All of this was a vast, long-overdue improvement of the entire judicial branch of government. I had been very supportive of that effort. When I was elected and took office in January 1975, most of the implementation under the Judicial Article had been accomplished.

Howell Heflin's Success

One aspect of this much needed constitutional reform was a retirement system for judges, and that resulted in many judges retiring. For example, there were three vacancies on the Supreme Court when I ran in '74 as a result of the retirement of elderly judges. I don't know of any efforts to repeal the entire Judicial Article, but judicial retirement is attacked almost annually. Critics charge that the retirement benefits are too generous, too costly. I don't know whether there has been any study undertaken but I do know that the current system, though a limited reform, is better than what we had before. The current legislature has passed legislation reducing judicial retirement benefits.

Arden: Once the very elderly judges were allowed to retire, and had access to retirement benefits, were they pleased to do so?

Janie: Yes. There was no resistance from them at all. They were pleased to have the option. The new constitution provided for a mandatory retirement age, an age beyond which one cannot run for re-election.

I joined the Court in a period of change, in personnel, procedure, and attitude. Of the nine justices, five were relatively new. The Chief Justice, Howell Heflin, had been elected only a few years earlier. This new group that eased the way for all of us.

The Court retained the tradition of sitting in divisions, which had been going on for years. Certain cases were heard and considered by the Court sitting *en banc*. Others cases were heard by one division that consisted of four justices plus the Chief Justice who sat on both divisions. The whole Court heard some cases, while others were heard by one of the divisions. Generally, one week out of the month was consumed with hearing oral arguments.

Creating the Court of Civil Appeals

In an effort to deal with an ever-increasing caseload, a Court of Civil Appeals of limited jurisdiction had been created. It had exclusive jurisdiction over domestic relations cases and limited jurisdiction over certain civil appeals. All criminal appeals went initially to the Court of Criminal Appeals.

The Supreme Court had discretionary review of the decisions of these courts by writ of *certiorari*. The writ was granted as a matter of right in death penalty cases, but other than that, Supreme Court review of decisions of these intermediate appellate courts is discretionary.

The Administrative Office of Courts was created to help with administrative tasks that by tradition had been exercised by the Chief Justice. This system had resulted in almost no uniformity with regard to timely disposition of cases, for example, by the trial courts. Each Circuit had its own rules, or no rules, with regard to disposition of cases. A survey of those courts showed that most worked very well in every respect, notwithstanding the fact that there was no oversight.

Perhaps because that was true, there was some resistance from some judges to the establishment of time standards; but for the most part, all of the justices and trial judges accepted the new procedures, and took pride in the positive national attention which Alabama got as a result of its new judicial system.

Justice is a Blind Docket

By long tradition, cases are assigned to each member of the Supreme Court on a rotating basis from a case pool called "blind docket." Justices had numbers from one to eight, and cases were assigned by the clerk's office to each of us using those numbers. In an effort to assign cases on as neutral, non-partisan a basis as possible, neither the justice nor the clerk's office knew to whom a case was assigned until the case number and the judge number were aligned.

There were no rules about how long a case remained undecided. Each justice handled his docket as he saw fit. I tried to decide a case assigned to me within a limited time, and never more than six months from the date of submission, but the pace of writing opinions varied widely among the justices.

There was also a wide variation among the justices in the use of law clerks. Some had a law clerk draft a proposed opinion with little or no discussion with the judge. Others directed the law clerk to draft a proposed opinion deciding the case one way or the other.

Some justices, as I did, set a self-imposed time frame in which to write an opinion. Most of the time that goal was reached, but not always. The caseload was such that no judge was ever caught up. All shared, in varying degrees, a sense of responsibility to decide the cases within a reasonable time.

Unlike the Supreme Court of the United States, most state supreme courts have no control over the number of cases that come before them. The volume of work is demanding, so we were constantly looking for ways to be more efficient. For example, for many years oral argument was granted in all cases if demanded by one of the parties. Each side was automatically granted thirty minutes to argue.

As the volume increased, this practice changed. We realized that not all cases required a full hour's oral argument, for example. Rather than having oral argument granted in every case in which a party requested it, the Court adopted a practice of assigning cases to a justice when ready for submission to determine, in his judgment, whether oral argument was warranted. He would then recommend either granting or denying oral argument.

No single judge made that determination, but his recommendation would be referred to a division, that may or may not accept it. More often than not, the recommendations were adopted by the Court without much debate.

Less Talk Leads to Less Deep Thought

As time wore on, fewer and fewer cases were accepted for oral argument. This practice resulted in more efficiency and dramatically reduced the number of cases in which the Court heard oral argument. I came to have misgivings about adopting that practice as fewer and fewer cases were heard orally. Without oral argument, cases might get decided more quickly but they don't receive sufficient exposure to the in-depth challenge that an oral argument can supply.

The practice differs from state to state. Some states don't encourage oral argument at all. Alabama has become more like that. In any event, because of Howell Heflin and his efforts to bring more efficiency to the judicial department, Alabama's court system received national attention, all favorable. This was a welcome change for the state.

Alabama was really ahead of the national curve on the whole notion of judicial modernization. Many changes were taking place when I came aboard, and I think it did ease the way for me. It would have been a much starker contrast had I joined the old Court, consisting of the same judges who'd been there 30 years.

As it happened, because retirements were now possible, I was not the only new member of the Court. Even so, institutionally I was a new phenomenon. Only two states had female justices then: Arizona and South Carolina. Both of these had been appointed, not elected. I was treated mostly like any other member but at first I got the impression sometimes that I constituted kind of a damper on casual conversation.

That didn't last long because in the end the only thing that mattered to all of us was the case before us. All of us wanted to decide the cases correctly, and while we had major disagreements, they were about the case we were considering. The other judges didn't give me any harder time than they gave anybody else in the debates.

In Janie's Opinions

I was not particularly aware of it, but when I retired my secretary told me that in all of the years I had been on the Court, I had not "lost" a case. She was referring to the fact that since the justices don't discuss cases before the conference where proposed opinions are presented and voted upon, the writer does not know whether the opinion will get a total of five votes.

Proposed opinions are first presented in Division Conference (four justices plus the Chief Justice) by the author of the opinion. The proposed opinion is discussed and votes are cast. Any one dissent means that the proposed opinion did not carry in Division and, therefore, must be taken to the full Court. A dissenting justice is expected to write a dissent for consideration at the General Conference where all nine vote. If the dissent attracts a total of five votes, the original dissenter is assigned the case and writes an opinion for the majority.

Many cases, of course, can be decided both ways, and all appeals at the final level of the appellate process are close. I tried to be sure that any opinion that I proposed was based upon a fair reading of the facts and an impartial application of the law.

What my secretary meant about my not losing was the fact that most of my opinions attracted the necessary four votes in Division and, if not, attracted at least five (including mine) in

General Conference. Sometimes it was necessary to change the law and overrule a case or a line of cases. That is part of the responsibility of a court of last resort which the supreme court is, but this is done on a very conservative basis.

Arden: On a personal level, how did you establish the operation of your office?

Janie: First of all, one of the things that dictated the way I managed my office was the fact that I never physically moved to Montgomery. As time passed, and as new judges were elected, fewer and fewer of them physically relocated to Montgomery.

Richard L. Jones and I were the first to establish offices outside of Montgomery. Cumberland Law School gave us office space, and we worked there along with our law clerks on a daily basis. We went to Montgomery as often as necessary, usually once or twice a week. From time to time, emergency matters would require us to change this schedule.

Later on, offices for us were made available at the local county courthouse. We were in Montgomery as often as need be, some weeks five days. Other times I was there only one day a week, depending on the Court calendar. Those of us who did not go to Montgomery every day kept a secretary and a law clerk in Montgomery.

Driving Janie

Judge Jones and I maintained an office in Birmingham, and each of us had one law clerk there. Part of his or her duty was to drive us back and forth to Montgomery as required, an hour-and-a-half drive at the most. It was not wasted time. I got lots of work done while being driven back and forth from Birmingham to Montgomery. I was very pleased with the mechanics of how my office worked.

Each judge's office is like a little law firm unto itself. There is very little interchange among all the judges on a daily basis. Each judge organized his office differently and used the law clerks differently. I am sure now, looking back, that I should have required more of the clerks. It would have been beneficial to them and to me.

Arden: What was your style?

Janie: Heflin used to say I didn't use my law clerks enough; that I didn't delegate enough to them. I am sure that is true. I didn't demand as much of them as I should have. Others felt perfectly comfortable with delegating quite a lot to law clerks. Of course, law clerks differed in their skills. Some were more helpful than others.

Arden: Did you interview your own law clerks or did somebody else do that for you?

Janie: Most of the time I interviewed them myself, but I don't think I had any more insight as to who would make a good law clerk as a result of personal interviews.

The overwhelming concern was getting the work out. In all of the years I was there, not a single judge was ever without a number of pending cases. The number varied, of course, but the caseload was such that everyone had a backlog.

For many years, the judges did not have law clerks. The clerk innovation helped, but by tradition a law clerk served for only one year and was just out of law school. For years, each judge had just one law clerk. I was among the last to hire two law clerks. A few judges had what was called a staff attorney who was more or less a permanent law clerk. I eventually had a staff attorney, too. There was no legislation or Court rule that required a law clerk to be retained for just one year. It was just a tradition.

Some of us, some really early on, found a law clerk that they were really compatible with and trusted and kept them indefinitely as staff attorneys. Like law clerks, they served only as long as the judge wanted them to. I am confident that having a permanent employee produced some real efficiency in a number of offices. The staff attorney became for some judges the mainstay in the office.

Arden: When was it that you hired or kept somebody on?

Janie: In the last term I served. I never had but one staff attorney in all the years I served, and that was in the last term. I don't think it was for the whole term. Some of the other judges had staff attorneys who served for many years.

A Day in the Life

Arden: When a case was assigned to you, how would you normally proceed?

Janie: I can describe my first day on the job, after the ceremonial part. Remember, previously I had worked as a law clerk to Judge Simpson, so I was not shocked to learn that a lot of work was involved. Still, even I was shocked when "my cases" were delivered in such huge volume to my office that first day on big rolling library tables.

In theory, cases are assigned to judges blindly. Each justice is assigned a number; each case is assigned a number; and assignments are made on a neutral blind rotation. Unlike the Supreme Court of the United States, cases are not discussed before assignment. Once a case is ready for submission, it is assigned to the next judge on the rotation. Everything in the case — transcript of the trial court record, briefs of the parties, all motions applied for and granted by the clerk's office — is then assigned to the judge next up on the list.

In those days, everything was on paper. Transcripts of the trial record were on transcript paper that was much bigger than standard-size legal paper. I once asked why transcripts were required to be on that paper and was told: "Because that is the size of the leather-bound books in which they are permanently bound." I decided not ask why the books were so big.

The delivery of your cases that first day on the job is an overwhelming sight. I worked on the cases by beginning with the oldest first, never did deviate from that rule. For various reasons, other members of the Court would approach the case assignment differently. Some would look through the pending cases and select some of the less-demanding ones to write first.

Some would do that in order to have a decent number of cases to present at the next conference. It was within the judge's discretion how to handle pending cases, as it was with law clerks. I found that it was more productive for me to start with the final order appealed from and then read the briefs. I would sometimes ask the law clerk to research specific questions that I might have that were not clear from the briefs.

Again, practice differed among the judges, but all of us felt the pressure of pending cases and the need to dispose of appeals in a timely manner.

We were all concerned about releasing opinions in a procedure that ensured that the outcome of a decision would become known simultaneously to all interested parties. Once a vote was taken in conference, great care was taken by the clerk to assure that knowledge of the decision was guarded until formally released.

Arden: Would you handle just one case at a time?

Janie: I would work on one case at a time, while the law clerk or clerks were working on others. At any one time, I might have 25 to 30 cases assigned to me. New ones were assigned as they were submitted.

Three of us came on the Court at the same time, replacing three retiring judges. I think we agreed to divide among ourselves all of the cases previously assigned to those retiring judges so that we had an equal number, rather than just transferring to us the pending cases of each of the retiring judges.

Arden: Let's say there were 25 cases in your closet. When you were working with them, did you just work on one at a time until it was resolved and was ready for conference, or did you work on a number of them?

Janie: I worked on a number of them but in different stages. I always selected the oldest one to work on next. Some of them I could look at, and after reading the final judgment and briefs, know what result likely was. I would tell my law clerk my preliminary impression, and direct him or her to read the briefs and record, independently research the law, and draft an opinion consistent with the law. I never started on a new case until I had reached a decision in the one I was working on.

Conference Room Procedure

Arden: When I asked if your being the only female on the Court made a difference in how normal business was conducted, you said you thought your presence inhibited conversation.

Janie: Especially at first, I think it did. But we all had a common desire to make Division Conferences and General Conferences move as smoothly as possible, and last only as long as necessary to handle the business. Division Conferences normally went pretty smoothly.

First, there were five judges involved instead of nine. But I noticed right away that there were basic ways we could reduce the time spent around the conference room table. For example, consider the physical arrangements. We sat around a big conference table, always in strict conformity with seniority.

Every arrangement was based upon seniority. The Chief Justice sat at the head of the table with the senior-most justice to his right, the next to his left, and so on down the table. The most junior member was at the end, on the left. No one else was allowed in the room unless called to enter.

Janie's Efficiency Reforms

To reduce the time spent around that table, I suggested some practical changes. Because every member was eager to improve efficiency, there was unanimous agreement to have the votes on proposed opinions collated and circulated to each justice before general conference. If a case had five or more votes, it did not require a long discussion to determine that the proposed opinion carried.

Prior to the adoption of this practice, there was no formal indication of whether the proposed opinion would become the Court's opinion. With votes circulated before conference, a dissent could be prepared, at least informally, and the discussion of the case clarified.

A uniform vote sheet was prepared, and the vote of each justice was recorded before conference. This required a central location for the votes to be recorded, and the vote sheet was circulated before conference. The time saved was a remarkable improvement.

Chief Justice finally agreed that his staff would be the central place to turn vote sheets in to one person. With this procedure, once we got in the conference, if the vote sheet showed that your proposed opinion had five votes, there was no need to spend any more time on it. Discussion of a case was never denied, and all questions were discussed, but a proposed opinion in which a majority agreed could be disposed of much quicker. Of course, any member could write a dissent.

Arden: What happened if there were judges who didn't know how they were going to vote?

Janie: A full discussion would take place. A proposed opinion would be defended by its author. Any judge could either concur, concur specially in writing explaining his vote, or he could simply dissent, or dissent in writing explaining his reasons.

Arden: Are you saying that with the votes circulated before conference, a prolonged discussion of each case was not necessary if the opinion had five votes?

Janie: Yes, that simple step shortened the time in conference enormously. The suggestion that we vote before meeting in conference was meant only to make conferences faster and smoother, but the suggestion did not affect presentation of a case by the individual judge. He or she can present it any way he wants. I hoped and tried to present the cases the best I could in the written opinion. Opinions were circulated well before the conference, so there was usually plenty of time to read and study them before voting, so I didn't elaborate much on the opinion itself.

I tried in conference to point out the arguments on the other side and to defend my reasons for concluding as I had done. I felt an obligation to point out that I had exercised judgment in reaching the conclusion that I recommended, and explain why I reached that conclusion. My presentations were probably shorter than anybody else's.

We did have one judge who would not add anything to what he wrote in his proposed opinion. He did not elaborate, but would answer any questions anyone had. He would simply say, "I've circulated my opinion; you can vote as far as I'm concerned." He saw no need to discuss a case beyond that.

Arden: Who was that?

Janie: That was Faulkner. But it was his prerogative to present his cases as he saw fit.

Arden: When you went to conference, had you already written a full opinion?

Janie: Yes, and circulated it well in advance so that there was time to read and study the opinion. Additional time to write a dissent was allowed if needed. Usually cases to be considered on a Monday conference were required to be circulated no later than the preceding Thursday.

General Conference was on the first Monday of the month. Division Conferences were on other Mondays. Division Conferences were usually preceded by a General Conference to consider any matter requiring the full Court. It was not unusual for General Conference to run into Tuesday or beyond. Weekends were spent studying opinions to be voted on during the coming week.

Arden: They expected you to work on weekends?

Janie: It was expected that you would be prepared to vote on proposed opinions the following week. You could study them anytime you wanted to as long as you didn't delay the process. Clement Clay Bo Torbert, who became Chief Justice after Heflin left the Court, once told me that he read my proposed opinions last, late on Sundays, because they were so clear he understood them even when he was very tired. I took that as a compliment.

Arden: Let's go back to the individual personalities on the Court. You want to tackle some of that and how you related to some of the people there and some of them who came on later?

Janie: When I came on, almost all of the justices were new to the Court. Only Justice Pelham Merrill remained of the older justices whom I had known when I clerked for Justice Simpson. I admired him greatly. As the senior-most judge, he headed the Merrill Division. Hugh Maddox, being the next senior, headed the Maddox Division. The Chief Justice sits on both divisions.

Seniority is Serious

When I was starting on the Court, three of us were going on at one time with no rule about who to swear in first in terms of seniority. I remember wondering what difference it would make if I were first, second, or third in terms of seniority. We were all going on at the same date; we were all going to be paid the same amount of money.

A friend suggested that I get the number that would gain me the most seniority because they wouldn't have that system if it didn't mean something. And he was right. Seniority determined what office you got, determined who got the next automobile, etc. I think it even included the pencils. Seniority meant everything.

Reneau Almon had been on the Court of Criminal Appeals when he ran for the Supreme Court so he knew about how the seniority system worked. He suggested that because of his prior service on that court, he should get the most senior position of the three of us coming in on the same day. I agreed, so Reneau and I decided that he would be first, I would be second, and we would tell Eric he was third. That's the way we did it. There were no hard feelings.

The Merrill Division

I wanted to be situated so that I would be assigned to Judge Merrill's division instead of Judge Maddox's division. I had known Judge Merrill from years ago clerking for Judge Simpson, and had great admiration for him.

To speed up the process and handle the maximum number of cases in the most efficient way, the Court years before had configured itself into two divisions, named for the two most senior judges, not counting the Chief Justice. When I came on, the Merrill division and the Maddox division sat separately. The Merrill division was known within the Court as the fast division. He worked hard and never got behind in all the years he was there. Being on his division suited me for a lot of reasons.

Assignment to the divisions was alternated with the most senior assigned to the Merrill division and so on down the line. Seniority mattered in every aspect, except it was applied in reverse for some functions. The most junior judge was first to vote and last to speak. Membership on a division shifts anytime there's a shift in the Court. But I never served on the other division. I was on the division headed by the senior-most judge the whole time I was there. I never served as head of a division because I never was the senior-most associate justice. This was because Reneau and I served exactly the same length of time, and we had agreed on the first day that he could be senior to me. It was purely a mathematical determination.

Five Votes Rule

Everybody preferred Division Conference to General Conference. First of all, there are only five judges participating as opposed to nine. Everything went faster. There was less acrimony, less of everything. While we did not always agree with a proposed opinion, sometimes differences about an opinion could be worked out in Division Conference without having to go to General Conference.

For example, if a proposed opinion received no concurring votes in Division Conference, it was unlikely that it would attract four votes in General Conference. In an instance like that, the opinion might be withdrawn and re-written deciding the case the other way. No one relished taking a case to General Conference having attracted only one or no concurrences in Division Conference.

Arden: When it came out of your division, would those normally come out with five votes or would there be a split?

Janie: Any case that came out of division with fewer than five votes went to General Conference, so almost always some cases went to General Conference from a Division Conference. That's as it should be. These are important cases or they would not have reached the Supreme Court. Many of them could be decided both ways, so it is not surprising that there were frequent disagreements about how to decide a case.

Arden: It didn't have to be presented at General Conference at all?

Janie: That is correct. An opinion with five votes becomes the vote of the Court. That, of course, is the result the author wanted and why the law clerks had a competitive attitude about the cases. If I came from Division Conference with a Court for all of my proposed opinions, the clerks were pleased to have "won all of our cases" and therefore have to go to General Conference. They became quite competitive about that.

Court Cast of Characters

Arden: Who was on the Court when you got there?

Janie: Howell Heflin was Chief Justice; Justices Pelham Merrill, Hugh Maddox, Jimmy Bloodworth, Richard "Red" Jones, and James Faulkner. The three of us who came on together, Eric Embry, Reneau Almon and I, made up the nine.

Arden: Did you know any of these people before you came on the Court?

Janie: Yes, I knew all of them.

Arden: What kind of relationships did you have?

Janie: I had known Red Jones for some time. He was a plaintiff's lawyer from Birmingham. After I was elected, Cumberland Law School offered me an office at the law school in Birmingham, and Red and I shared offices there. I'd known him for a couple of years. I had known Eric for probably longer than that.

I knew Judge Merrill, of course, from clerking for Judge Simpson. Jimmy Bloodworth and I had served on a committee together writing pattern jury instructions for years.

I had not known Reneau well but, like Jimmy Bloodworth, he had served on that same committee with me; and like Jimmy Bloodworth, he had been a circuit judge.

I would describe the Court as a compatible one. There were no acrimonious encounters of any sort and while we did not always agree, we remained a congenial group.

Arden: Did it remain that way?

Janie: It did. Although we disagreed vehemently sometimes on cases, the acrimony was generally limited to the conference room.

As time went on, and as the national campaign for the so called "tort reform" intensified, Jones, Faulkner, Embry, Almon, and I were later joined on the court by Mark Kennedy who came on after Judge Merrill retired. The Chief Justice often voted with us. We had a solid majority philosophically on the Court. Critics would say we were the liberals on the Court. I tended to reject that label. We followed the law, as did all of us, but we probably were more reluctant than some of the others to reject jury determination of issues.

Arden: The five of you who were the newest basically had a similar philosophy?

Janie: Heflin usually joined us and sometimes we got Judge Merrill.

Arden: Was it Maddox who was the most conservative?

Janie: Maddox was probably the most conservative of that first group and he remained so.

The 90s Conservative Sweep

Janie: The Court did not shift to a completely conservative position until after our group left. There was a concerted effort in the mid-to-late '90s to elect only conservative judges to state appellate courts. It began in Texas and travelled east through Louisiana, Mississippi, and Alabama.

Karl Rove actually came to the South with the express objective of electing more conservative judges to state courts. Conservatives nationwide were clamoring for "tort" reform, and Rove went about looking for conservative candidates to run against any judge considered to be liberal. He and his group selected candidates, and he actually managed those campaigns.

Up until then, political campaigns for judges had been very low key and did not involve a lot of money. For example, I spent only $34,000 on my first campaign. After Rove came south and politicized judicial races, it was not unusual for a campaign to cost millions of dollars. Also personal attacks on judges became as common as they are in any other political race.

Arden: Did that have any influence on your decision to run for another term?

Janie: It was certainly a factor. I believed I could have been reelected, but it would have been a bitter, expensive race.

Other factors also played a part in my decision not to run. One was my husband's health, but not the deciding one. After a lot of thought, after four terms, I finally decided not to run for another term.

Reneau had no hesitation. He decided early on that he would not run again. As it turned out, Reneau and I came on the Court at the same time and left at the same time. The big change in the Court's philosophy took place after I was gone, but the national movement to gain control of state courts was well underway. It was not totally completed until after I was gone.

The conservative philosophy permeating judicial elections was becoming nationwide, not just in Alabama but everywhere: Texas, Mississippi, Louisiana, and Missouri. Great sums of money were being devoted to judicial races.
I had never raised much money, nor spent much in my races. That was true in most court races. They did not include much television advertising, if any. To preserve fairness in court rulings, judges are supposed to be above partisan politics. Most bought some ads in newspapers, and some radio, but traditionally media campaigns were not often the deciding factor in court races.

Not Running for Impersonal Reasons

I was considering all of these factors and was still ambivalent. Howell Heflin, then in the U. S. Senate, came and we talked. He urged me to give some real thought to not running. He said, "Right now you've got an impeccable judicial record, no blemishes of any sort, but you won't be able to come out of this race with that."

He knew more about what was happening than I did and about the questionable campaign tactics. He told me that Karl

Rove was coming to Alabama with unlimited money to spend on judicial races and that my race would be a sure target of that conservative group.

The year 1998 was the beginning of what became the norm: millions of dollars spent on judicial races.

Arden: Karl Rove managed the whole thing, and it was a complete sweep?

Janie: Republicans won every seat.

Arden: Do you think you'd have been a victim of that?

Janie: I think I might have been able to pull it off, but it would have been awfully expensive, and my supporters didn't have that kind of money. I would have been harder to beat than some of the others if the debate had been honest.

Mark Kennedy, a fine lawyer, won his election to another term in spite of Rove and his smear campaign. (In an interesting twist of fate, he later married Peggy, George Wallace's liberal daughter.) At that time, many rumors were spread by the opposition. Mark was accused of being a pedophile in distorted reference to his charity work with abused children over the years. Judicial campaigns were no longer conducted differently from ruthless political ones.

The result for all our election races today is obvious.

Janie as legal secretary, Mobile, Alabama

Janie marrying
Bill Ellzey

Vincent Fonde Kilborn, Jr.

Women who attended University of
Alabama School of Law with Janie

JUST CALL ME JANIE

Janie's Profile from Law School

Janie's early years

Janie with Daughter at work

Janie with Helen Vance

Howell Heflin swearing in Janie to Al. Supreme Court

Janie in Office

Janie Shores

Section Three

Reforms

JUST CALL ME JANIE

JANIE SHORES

REFORMS

"IN ALL CRIMINAL PROSECUTIONS, THE ACCUSED SHALL ENJOY THE RIGHT TO A SPEEDY AND PUBLIC TRIAL, BY AN IMPARTIAL JURY."
U.S. CONSTITUTION, BILL OF RIGHTS, AMENDMENT VI

CONTENTS

INTERVIEW VII – 1/19/2011: JUSTICE IS TRIAL BY JURY
PAGE 199

INTERVIEW VIII – 2/2/2011: SHE NEVER LOST A CASE
PAGE 213

PHOTOS
PAGE 229

Just Call Me Janie

Interview VII

Justice is Trial by Jury

Janie: I don't know exactly how many opinions I wrote over the years, but I tried to write one a week. In addition, there are *certiorari* petitions from the Court of Civil Appeals and Court of Criminal Appeals. The Supreme Court reviews all of the petitions and may or may not grant the writ.

Each justice is assigned those petitions on a blind rotating basis and recommends to the Court either to grant or deny them. If granted, a full opinion follows as in cases appealed.

Although I worked to keep my docket current, I never at any time got caught up. There were always cases waiting to be studied.

The Alabama Supreme Court is a high-volume Court. There is no overall way to control the volume of cases. A partial solution has been to create the two lower appellate courts and make the Supreme Court solely a *certiorari* court. Alabama has not done that entirely, but it's a *certiorari* court in criminal cases and in civil cases, up to a certain amount in controversy, and in domestic relations cases.

The creation of two lower courts lightens the load of the Supreme Court by limiting the kinds of cases it can hear and offering a little discretion in what kinds of cases are reviewable in the Supreme Court.

Arden: What caused the movement to get more conservatives elected to the courts, not just in Alabama, but elsewhere?

The Jury System Under Siege

Janie: Basically, a distrust of the jury system. I make no apology for believing in the jury system. But the campaign to elect more conservative judges was often based upon distrust of the jury system in civil cases. Big money judgments in civil cases were always cited as a reason calling for "tort reform."

Many conservatives don't like laws, like Alabama's, that allow a jury to determine the amount of damages that are appropriate to redress wrongs.

I support the constitutional jury system. I do believe that the jury system is one reason the general public continues to believe that the civil justice system provides a remedy for conduct resulting in injury to them. I believe public confidence in our system of justice rests largely on a belief that the system affords a fair method of resolving disputes. I think the opposite view is distrust of any system that does not permit a way to calculate cost of behavior before it is taken.

The fundamental reason for the effort to elect politically conservative judges was dislike for that system. The attack on the judiciary and the drive to elect different judges was in truth an attack on the jury system in civil cases often framed as "tort reform." Those of us who strongly and consistently insisted upon the right of a jury to decide things, mostly things involving money, were branded as liberals and targeted for defeat at the first opportunity.

I disagree with the liberal label in this issue. I think ours was a very conservative philosophy. After all, the right of trial by jury was one of the first rights enumerated in the Constitution. Most people look on adhering to the premises of the original U.S. Constitution and other ideas of the 1700s as conservative. I always liked the way it first was expressed, that the right of trial by a jury shall remain "inviolate." That's pretty direct and clear.

I suppose any system that does not permit the calculation of cost for behavior in advance is distrusted. It is difficult to estimate the cost of doing business if that includes the discretion of twelve citizens asked to determine a monetary amount to punish for behavior that results in harm to another. I think that is basically what drives the never-ending challenge to the jury system in civil cases. The tension between the civil justice system and business interests increases as juries return verdicts in greater amounts.

Those who oppose jury discretion look for ways to instill certainty. They look to the legislature, but the remedy there is limited to what the Constitution permits. It guarantees a trial by jury. This tension has been going on since the system was devised. This tension is constant but, increasingly, in recent years there have been efforts to get relief in the courts.

Those challenging punitive damages in civil cases often based the argument on the uncertainty of jury determinations. The argument that this uncertainty amounts to lack of due process was advanced time and again. It was expressed in various ways, but at the base of the argument is the inability to factor in the cost of the activity involved when jury discretion is a component. More and more effort was made to get the Supreme Court of the United States to establish standards limiting jury discretion in these civil cases.

For quite a long time, that Court did not take up the issue, but as more conservative judges came onto the Court, it finally agreed to take up the issue. They started to take some of these cases, and although the Court did not hold that jury discretion in such cases violated the due process clause *per se*, it hinted that there could be circumstances under which unbridled jury discretion could amount to failure of due process. These early cases were a warning to the states that jury discretion awarding punitive damages in civil cases was limited by the Federal Constitution's due process guarantee.

That raises other interesting questions. Due process is generally thought to include some idea of your potential exposure, some notice of what your exposure might be if you commit certain acts. In the criminal law context, statutes must, to meet due process standards, state with some certainty the penalty for violating those standards. Those standards need not, in the criminal law context, be precise. Countless criminal penalties are expressed in terms that are very general. One penalty may be fines varying from small amounts to great sums. Statutes providing for incarceration upon conviction may leave to the Court the term of the sentence, from a very short term to very long terms. You can get anywhere from a one-year sentence to a life sentence in many instances.

Is that lack of due process? That's what the legislature has prescribed as an appropriate punishment. The jury decides more often than not which degree of a crime the defendant is guilty of, and then the judge sentences accordingly, often within a range of punishment.

There was enough indication from the Supreme Court that punitive damages in civil cases might, depending upon the facts, violate the Constitution. With this warning, I wrote an opinion that established a procedure for trial courts when a punitive damage award was challenged as being excessive. We established a requirement that trial courts have a hearing and determine that issue. Courts were required to consider all relevant facts of this issue. How does the punitive damage amount compare to the compensatory damages? How did this award compare to other jury awards in like cases? What are any other facts that might shed light on the issue?

In short, we established a requirement that the trial courts hold a hearing on the specific issue so the factors it considered would be included in the record on appeal; thus, a reviewing court would have the information about agreed-on basics when reviewing a challenge to the jury award on constitutional grounds. The Supreme Court, in an opinion written by Justice Blackmun, affirmed this with six members of the Court holding that the procedure that Alabama had adopted satisfied due process requirements and that punitive damages are allowable and do not *per se* violate due process.

I suspect that most states have adopted some form of due process review to test punitive verdicts when challenged under due process, either by a formal way or less formally as we did.

Arden: Did this help to solidify punitive damages?

Janie: I believe so. This case answered the question of whether in civil cases the award of punitive damages *per se* violated the due process requirements of the Constitution. I think the law is pretty well settled now.

Arden: What was the most controversial opinion you authored?

Janie: I don't know, but I do remember one I wrote shortly after joining the Court that got a lot of attention. I held that an old statute requiring a husband to sign a deed conveying real estate solely in the wife's name was invalid and unconstitutional. It was one of those laws based upon the assumption that a woman was incapable of handling her own affairs and, therefore, her husband's consent was necessary to protect her interests.

A Case of Equal Protection

The woman in the case had agreed to sell real estate solely in her name and entered into an agreement to do so. She changed her mind and refused to execute a deed when the buyer attempted to consummate the agreement. The woman, who was the seller and who had signed the agreement to convey the property, attempted to void the agreement on the ground that her husband had not signed the agreement to sell in accordance with the statute. She had simply changed her mind about selling the property but she tried to defend the case brought by the buyer on the basis of that old statute.

The holding was that the statute was in violation of the Constitution's guarantee of equal protection under the law and hence void; thus the decision eventually went against the wife in this case, whose interests the statute was theoretically designed to protect.

This old statute was based upon the presumption that a married woman was incapable of protecting her own interests and, therefore, her husband's consent was required before she could alienate her property. In this case, the wife relied on that statute as a defense to a suit brought by the purchaser seeking to compel her to live up to her part of the bargain. I wrote an opinion that held that that statute was unconstitutional as applied to allow her to escape the obligations of the contract she made. A majority of the Court agreed, and the statute was voided.

The opinion got a lot of public attention not only because it invalidated a law that had been around a long time, but because the first woman ever elected to the Court was the author of the opinion, and also because the result went against the wife in this case.

Arden: The wife in this case was hiding behind the statute.

Janie: She was taking advantage of it. The conclusion was that the statute was unconstitutional as a denial of equal protection of the laws based on the gender of the party.

Arden: Was that a liberal interpretation of the law or conservative?

Janie: Neither.

Arden: I didn't think so. Were there any judges who dissented?

Janie: Yes. And it was legitimate legal dissent. At least two of the justices felt that since the legislature passed the law to protect a wife's interests, and it's a policy decision, it was within the authority of the legislature to do that, and if the policy behind it was to be changed, it should be left to the legislature. This is a legitimate argument. After all, it was the legislature that decided that a woman should have the protection of her husband's counsel before alienating her property. That idea goes back to times in pre-Revolutionary England when women couldn't own property at all.

The dissent made the point that the holding put in jeopardy every law regulating marital property rights which treats husband and wife differently, or treats the husband differently from single persons. It points out that after this decision, a wife may convey her separate property free of any marital encumbrance.

On the other hand, the husband cannot convey his separate and real property without encumbrance unless his wife is willing to join the conveyance because of his wife's potential dower interest in his estate. The dissent argued that the decision could lead to a holding that marital property rights established by the legislature are unconstitutional.

Court Rules Solely on Issues Presented

This possibility may be true, but dower interests and other marital rights were not the disputed issues before us. And we in the Court are charged to decide only the issue before us. We will decide those issues when and if they are presented in another case.

Again, the dissent has a point. But it is a dissent. One of the nicest things about writing a dissent is that you can say anything you want to.

Arden: You can say anything you want?

Janie: And make all of these dire predictions as to what's going to happen if this becomes the law. This particular issue got a lot of attention.

Arden: When something like this happens, do you personally get a lot of attention? Do you ever hear from the parties themselves?

Janie: Not often. You hear from the lawyers not infrequently. And sometimes people either involved in the case or ones who have had similar experiences will write letters.

Arden: Do you get letters from unconnected citizens? On something like this, there would be a lot of men in Alabama who I'm sure would have been irate about this conclusion that women can make their own decisions.

Janie: Yes. I'm sure there were.

Arden: They thought they had control over their wives and their wives' separate property, etc.

Janie: It is unusual for a layperson to get in touch with the Court, or more accurately, with an individual justice. But if there was that real interest in a case, there might be others joining in a motion for rehearing.

Occasionally, you get letters from the people involved. Just thanking you.

Labeling Myself

Arden: Would you describe yourself as a judge as being liberal or conservative?

Janie: My self-description might be different from that of an observer. I would describe myself as neither.

I believe profoundly in the jury system. I think the notion that a lay jury is the most appropriate way to determine facts in civil and criminal litigation is one of the most admirable features of our system. As I've said, public confidence in the judicial system in this country must be maintained, and it is very fragile.

What is the alternative to the civil justice system? What kind of country would we have if people did not believe that it offered a remedy for what are often grievous wrongs done to them?

I think it is very valuable to have a litigious society. What is the alternative? Our system may not be not very efficient; it is a case-by-case solution often; but I think it is very healthy for people to believe that they can get justice in their individual case by going to court.

They can also petition the legislature, or Congress, but that process is very slow, and the influence is uneven. There are very few lobbyists in state capitols and Washington working day to day on behalf of the people.

The Dangers of Current Tort Reform

If we don't hold on to the individual's right to trial by jury, the consequences will change the character of our country and our lives. So I defend that principle. But I seem to be losing the argument because the likes of Karl Rove and others supporting the concept of so-called "tort reform" and supporting only judges whom they believe will decide cases on the basis of their so-called 'conservative' philosophy are prevailing in state after state and even more significantly, perhaps, in the Supreme Court.

I have always, perhaps simplistically, believed that with proper information people were perfectly capable of electing honest people with integrity to the judiciary. I am becoming more and more skeptical about that. With unlimited money spending allowed in judicial campaigns, its influence cannot be denied. Again, Karl Rove proved that. And it has not taken long to see results.

One of the comforting features about the judicial system is that many, and I hope most, judges cannot be identified before they begin deciding cases as either liberal or conservative. Did you know that Hugo Black a U.S. Supreme Court justice known for his pro-Civil Rights stance was from the state of Alabama?

Arden: Yes.

Janie: He never went to law school. He read law; he didn't go to law school.

Arden: I remember that, too. He was quite an impressive person.

Janie: He really was. His son Hugo Jr. came back to Birmingham after a long absence and after his father died, but he found that the state has become too conservative to be welcoming to him. He left and went to Miami to practice.

You know, the terms "liberal" and "conservative" can get too confusing in describing judges. Sometimes following the Constitution gets one branded a liberal, and other times it is the opposite. Depends upon what kind of case it is.

Arden: Exactly. And whose interest it treads on. Do you have recollections from the Court that you would like to talk about?

Janie: I decided not to run again in 1998. Those of us who were branded liberal state judges now were targeted for elimination from office by well-funded, ultra-right-wing conservatives. That fact, plus personal reasons, gave me great pause about what could have been a fifth term. As it turned out had I run and won I would have been lonely in dissent, I'm afraid, for the next six years because the "tort reform conservatives" took over the Court.

Arden: Didn't somebody go on the Court that you and he kind of butted heads all the time?

Janie: No, because I was gone by the time the tort reform conservatives took over. But there were conservatives on the Court with whom I served the entire time I was there. We didn't exactly butt heads, but Hugh Maddox was probably the most consistent in voting on the conservative side of any issue. I'm not being critical. I'm sure he believed it, and I am sure he believed the law was on his side. But he and I almost inevitably came down on opposite sides of cases that involved what could be described liberal vs. conservative in resolution. Hugh and I just had different philosophies.

Running Lurleen Wallace

Maddox had been legal advisor to George Wallace in one of his early terms as governor. When Wallace had served his maximum terms in office and was not allowed to succeed himself, he kept political control by running his wife Lurleen for governor. Lurleen Wallace was elected and she appointed Hugh to the Court. Hugh and I differed in our views on a number of subjects. We were polar opposites politically.

Arden: Was there any personal animosity between you two?

Janie: No, not at all.

Arden: Ideological all the time?

Janie: Right, and the judges had very little social interchange anyway. We were together always on matters of business as opposed to social occasions. But even that being said, I didn't have animosity toward any of them. I was simply more philosophically compatible with some more than others.

Judge Merrill's Last Case

Arden: Did you ever feel that there was any personal animosity towards you within the court?

Janie: I don't think so. Judge Merrill, the senior-most judge with whom I served, and I liked him, having known him since I was a law clerk, dissented in a case I wrote once. And he said he'd never dissent from anything I wrote again because it was so hard to find flaws in my legal opinion.

It was the case I mentioned in which I held that the legislature had many years ago authorized civil suits against municipalities and the Court had simply ignored the statute for years. My opinion did not represent judicial activism at all. In fact, it represented just the opposite. It deferred to the legislature. Judge Merrill and the others who joined him in dissent were concerned about the impact the decision would have on local municipalities. The dissenters could not deny that the legislature had passed a law allowing citizens injured by a municipality to sue for damages. So in a sense, I was the conservative in holding that a person injured by a city employee could recover damages in a suit against the city.

I don't normally remember cases by the style of the case but that one was *Jackson vs. City of Florence*. The plaintiffs alleged that police officers in the City of Florence had injured the plaintiff while arresting him for some minor offense. The attorneys sued the City of Florence alleging that police officers had assaulted, willfully and wantonly, an unarmed 75-year-old 130-pound man. The lawsuit alleged that the police officers used excessive force in arresting the man, resulting in the loss of his right eye. He sued the City of Florence seeking damages for the injury done him.

The suit alleged that the plaintiff was arrested and taken to a small room at police headquarters, where he was beaten by the police and lost an eye. The plaintiff did not sue the officers; he sued the city. I held that if the allegations of the complaint were proven, the city could be held liable. Although one could not maintain an action against a city for the performance of governmental functions, police brutality is hardly the exercise of a governmental function. Sounds familiar today, doesn't it?

Judge Merrill's concern that allowing such suits might create too heavy a financial burden on cities might have been well taken. I thought there was no question that the officers were acting in an official capacity.

It's Bill Clinton's Office Calling

Arden: Tell me about being considered for an appointment to the Supreme Court of the United States.

Janie: Well, I was considered for a moment. One day, I was outside in my garden digging in the dirt. Sometimes when I'm trying to figure out a position on a case, I like to take a break and work outside. It clears my mind. The phone rings, and when I answer, I hear, "The White House calling."

It was Bernie Nussbaum who was Bill Clinton's legal advisor. He told me that I was being considered for the appointment, based upon a recommendation to the President from Senator Heflin. Nussbaum opened the conversation by saying jokingly, "Senator Heflin says that you are the smartest woman in Alabama."

I replied in the same joking spirit, "I hesitate to disagree with a senior senator."

Bernie Nussbaum told me that the process would move very fast and that the first thing I should do was to have a physical examination to provide a doctor's certification that my health was good. He advised me to get that out of the way first. He also said to be sure that I had no tax problems because tax problems were the most common stumbling blocks to political appointments.

I assured him that I did not have tax problems. I knew that to be true because I had not filed a joint return with Jim since Geraldine Ferraro had tax problems. She had filed a joint return with her husband when she was on the ticket for Vice President to Dukakis in his ill-fated run for President. She didn't have a tax problem, but her husband was alleged to have one. Since they had filed a joint return, his problem became hers.

In preparation for consideration for the U.S. Supreme Court, I was interviewed by the FBI. The process lasted about a week. Later, Senator Heflin called to tell me that President Clinton had appointed Ruth Ginsberg, a New Yorker who had been recommended by Senator Pat Moynihan.

I knew Ruth Ginsberg and had been on programs with her. I was disappointed that my consideration did not last long but I have been enormously proud of her.

INTERVIEW VIII

SHE NEVER LOST A CASE

Arden: You said that you never lost a case. What does that mean in terms of your time on the Alabama Supreme Court?

Janie: I mean that I never submitted a proposed opinion to the Court that did not eventually get a majority. One dissent in division takes a case to the full Court, to what we called General Conference. I never had a case that did not get five votes when it was taken to General Conference.

It is probably helpful to understand that, unlike the Supreme Court of the United States, we in the Alabama State Supreme Court did not discuss cases before they were assigned to a justice. That, of course, would be helpful in that you would get a general impression of how each judge was leaning in a case. But because we did not do that, opinions were written before they were to be considered by the Court. Sometimes, after oral argument, there would be informal indications as to how a judge might be leaning, but there was no formal conference for that purpose.

The reason for this procedure was the heavy caseload. It would just take too much time to meet and discuss each case.

The Supreme Court of the United States hears oral argument and then meets to discuss the case. Before an opinion is written, they take tentative votes, and the Chief Justice then assigns one of the justices in the majority to write the opinion for the Court.

That procedure is preferable to the one we used, but again, ours was dictated by the heavy caseload. Of course, one had an impression of how an individual judge was likely to vote in a given case, but that was all it was – an impression. Even so, it was not that difficult to anticipate how a judge would be likely to vote.

When I was there, we did not have a split in the Court that remained as predictable as the current U.S. Supreme Court. One almost knows beforehand how each of them will vote in a particular case.

Arden: Would you have enjoyed being a trial judge?

Janie: I think I am by nature best suited for an appellate court as opposed to a trial court.

Arden: Your temperament is well suited to the Supreme Court.

Janie: I think my kind of scholarship, my kind of interests, were most suited for appellate work. I enjoyed teaching for that reason, too. I enjoyed the classroom aspect of it more than writing law review articles. I like to write and I like it particularly when it has an immediate effect.

As I drafted opinions, in addition to monitoring clarity I was always mindful that the opinions had to be persuasive. First, in order to get consensus on the Court, but also to show the litigants that their arguments had been carefully considered, that a decision was reached in a thoughtful and deliberate manner.

I also found that teaching law school was a very good preparation for being on an appellate court. What you do there is so similar to court work. You spend all your time analyzing cases and trying to make the law make sense to a lay audience and students.

Arden: Did the Court change dramatically as new people were elected?

Janie: It changed with each new justice, but there was not a dramatic change until after I left. I served under four different Chief Justices.

There was Howell Heflin, who accomplished great things for the judicial system; he achieved constitutional change After he left to run for the U.S. Senate, Bo Torbert was elected. Their personalities were very different, but each made significant contributions to the Court.

Bo Torbert Boosts a Building

Bo Torbert had served many years in the State Senate and because of his good relations there he was able to persuade the legislature to support the building of a new judicial building.

For many years, the Court sat in a structure that had been used for a lodge of some sort. It had been adequate, but not impressive. Bo managed to get support for a proper judicial building within the capitol complex, and it was a significant achievement.

When Bo left, Ernest "Sonny" Hornsby was elected Chief Justice.

The Civil Rights Movement and the Civil Rights Act of the 1960s was the beginning of the departure of many white voters from the Democratic side to the Republican side. The surge in the Republican Party in Alabama began with the passage of the Voting Rights Act and continued to grow.

After a century of Democratic preference, the voters' party of choice changed. This party shift was driven by the same issue that made the Democrats the choice of the majority of Southern voters following the Civil War: race.

After Bo left the Court, Ernest "Sonny" Hornsby was elected Chief Justice. When he ran for re-election, he had

Republican opposition from a lawyer identified with the Republican Party.

Karl Rove Helps Elect Perry Hooper

Perry Hooper had been chairman of the state Republican Party at a time when there were few Republicans in the state. I knew who he was from that association rather than as a Montgomery lawyer, later elected as probate judge and then circuit judge. The result of the Chief Justice race was so close that a formal contest of the election was filed, and Hooper was finally declared the winner by just a few votes, fewer than 300, as I recall.

The Republican Party launched a determined effort to win control of the judicial systems in the South, beginning with the appellate courts. After achieving success, first in Texas, Mississippi, and other Southern states, Rove came to town to duplicate that success in Alabama. Electing Hooper as Chief Justice was one of his successes.

Hooper recently acknowledged that he would not have won without Rove's help in a letter to the editor of the *Montgomery Independent*. He gave Winton Blount, III part credit for his victory, saying, "He reached out to Karl Rove and brought him to Alabama, for which I am eternally grateful." In a notable understatement he wrote that, "Karl became instrumental in my successful election as Alabama's first Republican Chief Justice."

After long consideration and a lot of discussion, Sonny Hornsby decided not to appeal that decision, and Perry Hooper became the Chief Justice.

Despite a long, close campaign, he was welcomed to the Court. He was a friendly, amicable man, and there was not any hostility to him that I ever observed.

Harold See was also elected as a Republican. He was the only member of the Court in my years there to ever question the integrity of another justice who disagreed with him.

In just a few years, Republicans dominated the Court.

The Last Democrat

Arden: Are there any Democrats on the Court now?

Janie: No. Sue Bell Cobb was the last Democrat on the Court. She was elected Chief Justice as a Democrat. She did not complete her term but instead resigned before her term was over, allowing the Republican governor to fill the vacancy, which of course he did with a Republican to replace her. Now there are no Democrats on the Court. In fact, there is not one Democratic statewide office holder in Alabama.

The Republican Chief Justice appointed to replace Sue Bell was defeated by Roy Moore. Moore was trying to get elected to a full term. He was a circuit judge from Gadsden, Etowah County, and was well known to us on the Court because we'd had cases from time to time involving Judge Moore.

Moore displayed a plaque of the Ten Commandments as described in the Christian Bible behind the bench facing the courtroom. Some litigants filed a complaint objecting to this being displayed in the courtroom because judges are supposed to keep their religious beliefs private in order to respect other people's rights to freedom of religion. When that case reached the Supreme Court, we issued an order requiring him to remove the plaque, and I assume he did.

Some years later, he was elected to be Chief Justice. Among the first things he did was to eliminate the offices that some of us former justices maintained to help with extra work and emergency matters. These were spaces in the county courthouses that did not cost the state anything and they had been put to good work use by justices for many years.

Red Jones and I did much work for the Court from one of those offices in Birmingham, and I think there was one in Tuscaloosa. Red did a lot for the Court after he retired. It was not a budget-driven decision. The county provided those offices without cost to the state, and for a long time, by my choice, I was not compensated for the work I did.

The first thing Roy Moore did was to abolish those offices and end the important work that Red and I had been doing for the Court.

Media Coverage for Roy Moore

Arden: Why did Roy Moore, the newly elected Chief Justice, take away your offices?
Janie: Well, there was a lot of rancor; he knew we were among the ones who had voted against him.
Arden: So it was retribution?
Janie: It certainly wasn't Christian charity. Anyway, we went peaceably.

Moore made nationwide news with his attempts to gain media coverage when, not long after assuming office as Chief Justice, he moved that huge, heavy Ten Commandments monument into the new judicial building one night after hours.

The new court building was very handsome and a long time coming. We are all very proud of it. It was designed and did include a security system that the old building lacked. The new building included underground parking requiring a security code to enter, and the entrances and exits were secure, unlike the old building.

Bo had appointed me to be the Court representative with the architectural team on "decorative" matters, such things as floor coverings, etc. I never interfered with any decision the architectural group made but I was aware that the concern Bo had was with cost overruns. Any cost overrun was unrelated to decoration. The state-of-the-art security system, which everybody agreed was imperative, was not inexpensive.

When the news broke that Roy Moore had somehow, in the middle of the night, moved a several-hundred-pound monument of the Ten Commandments into the building, my second thought – and you can guess the first – was how on earth he got into the building past all of the security.

It was later disclosed that he had ordered the night watchman to leave the door unlocked. The plaque was pushed and pulled by several men into the building on a dolly of some kind via the handicap ramp.

None of the justices were informed beforehand. They discovered it in the building the next morning. There it sat in the rotunda. Some said that Chief Justice Moore had given the night watchman the night off and supervised the process himself.

By whatever means, the Chief Justice directed its installation. This whole act was against U.S. federal law. The illegal plaque stayed in the judicial building until Myron Thompson, United States District Judge, Middle District of Alabama, ordered its removal. When the Chief Justice defied this direct order of a United States District Court, he was, after a hearing, removed from office.

Alabama the Unconstitutional

It became another embarrassing public relations disaster for the state of Alabama. For years, the state has been held up to public ridicule as a result of George Wallace and his vows to maintain segregation in the state by screaming, "Segregation now; segregation tomorrow; segregation forever." Sadly, that pledge got him elected governor four times.

Roy Moore's defiance of a valid court order cost him his seat as Chief Justice. In spite of this, a few years later he was again elected Chief Justice. He now continues to bring ridicule on the state by defying and directing probate judges not to issue marriage licenses to same-sex couples, even after a federal judge ruled to the contrary. Again, Moore is facing disciplinary action. Complaints have been lodged against him in the Judicial Inquiry Commission, which operates rather like a grand jury. If the inquiry finds that there are reasonable grounds for sanctions, his case will go to the Court of the Judiciary.

He continues to bring negative national attention to Alabama.

Arden: Despite all the hard work that had gone into creating a good judicial system.

Camelot Court

Janie: When Heflin successfully promoted an amendment to the 1901 state constitution and achieved its implementation, Alabama was heralded as having one of the best judicial systems in the country just a few years ago. Howell Heflin's leadership and hard work deserve the credit for that. There was no trick to it. It was just persuading people that it can be done, showing them how it can be done, and getting them enthusiastic about doing something positive, and they did.

Some of the circuit judges got very inspired and started doing things they hadn't done in years to move cases along and handle things more expeditiously.

One of the biggest struggles had been getting the judges to adopt some time standards, to strive to move cases along.

Some judges resisted this, but others were willing to do so. It varied by personality. Some were very proud of the fact that they handled their dockets properly and efficiently, but they resisted being told to do so.

There is merit on both sides. All agreed that it was desirable to move cases along, but some resisted being required to report to the administrative agency. After all, trial judges are elected and most work hard to serve the public efficiently. After some resistance at first, it is my impression that the system is now running smoothly. Howell Heflin deserves credit forever for getting them to do that

Arden: So did you and the other Alabama judges force Roy Moore to take out the Ten Commandments plaque?

Janie: I didn't, the Federal Court did. It took a federal order to get him, a supposed officer of the law, to take it out.

Arden: Unbelievable.

Janie: I often wonder where that big stone monument is as we speak.

Arden: During your entire time on the Court was there ever another woman there?

Janie: No.

Arden: Now there are how many women on the Supreme Court?

Janie: I think there are three women on the appellate courts. But not a Democrat among them.

High Cost of Campaigns

After having seen both systems in use, it has become more difficult to defend the partisan election of judges.

I once believed that, properly educated about the system, voters would be qualified to select judges by popular vote, just as they do legislators, etc. Lay jurors every day decide issues of life and death in the trial courts and generally do so thoughtfully and fairly.

Now, with Citizens United, the Supreme Court has allowed unlimited money to be spent in political campaigns, including judicial campaigns. The money that goes into judicial races is absolutely obscene. Millions were spent in the last race for Chief Justice. I compare this to our races in the '70s in which I spent around $34,000.

Arden: What would you replace the system with?

Janie: I've never been convinced that the so-called Missouri method produces any better judges than our old system of letting the people decide. The Koch brothers and other wealthy campaign donors can have much too much influence on elections, and the results often do not represent the majority of voters. Our old system would still suit me fine if we could somehow take the big money out of it.

I just find it difficult to believe that inspite of the fact that the people can be trusted to make judgments of life and death and do that almost every day somewhere in America that somehow they can't be trusted to make decisions with respect to electing honest, qualified judges. Popular elections might still work if we could figure out a way to eliminate the influence of big money.

Some of the larger counties have adopted a system based upon the Missouri plan to fill vacancies on the trial courts when a sitting judge retires or dies. A panel of lawyers is appointed to send three names to the governor from which he is asked to select one to fill the vacancy. We have, or had, such a plan in Jefferson County.

One story, whether true or not, exposes the frailty of such plans. A vacancy occurred in Birmingham's Jefferson County during one of the Wallace administrations. The select panel of lawyers met and duly selected from a number of applicants three names to be sent to the governor from which to fill the vacancy. After failing to do so after two such submissions, Wallace is said to have told the Birmingham lawyers that they could keep sending three names, but until *his* choice for the vacancy was among them, he would make no selection.

Arden: That's the Wallace way to handle it.

Good Guys Don't Run

Janie: A major problem now in politics is that good people are so disheartened by the ugliness of campaign tactics that they rarely run. Few people see running for public office as the noble pursuit it is meant to be. Most people who run have a personal taste for gaining power even at the cost of dishonesty and destruction, with no interest in benefitting the public.

As far as political parties go, I'm profoundly Democratic; however, the process of getting elected makes it almost impossible not to be corrupted by special interest donors.

Arden: Do you have any hope for solving the big issues, such as the mega cost of campaigns and the false information circulated about policies and people?

Janie: I believe that the American people will eventually demand better politicians. In spite of widespread media distortion of facts and much political corruption, I believe that all people have a fundamental sense of fairness even in the face of misinformation. People eventually figure out when they are being lied to and mistreated. Our human desire for truth and basic sense of justice cannot be repressed forever.

Special Courts

Arden: Are you involved at all in the Court now?

Janie: No. Not in any formal way. From time to time there are enough recusals to require an appointment of some special court to sit on a particular case

For example, a special court had to be appointed when Roy Moore, then Chief Justice, was sanctioned by the U. S. District Court and ordered to remove his Ten Commandments monument from the judicial building. When he refused to do so, the case went to the Judicial Inquiry Commission. This is rather like a grand jury that hears cases against judges. If the Judicial Inquiry determines, after hearing the evidence, that the case should proceed, it goes to the Court of the Judiciary. If that court finds the accused guilty, an appeal to the Supreme Court may be taken.

In Roy Moore's case, all of the members of the Supreme Court recused themselves, for the obvious reason: they had all served with him when he was Chief Justice. Their participation in his appeal would have had the appearance of impropriety.

In that case, after all members of the Court recused themselves, a special court was convened consisting of retired judges from around the state. I sat on that court, along with retired judges from the court of criminal appeals, the circuit courts, etc. Full recusal happens infrequently, and the appointment of a special court is provided for in those instances.

Of course, it is not unusual for a single justice to recuse in a case. Usually, this does not require the appointment of a substitute judge, since there are more than five qualified judges remaining to hear the case.

Arden: Does this happen frequently?

Janie: No. It is unusual for the whole court to recuse. But it is not unusual for one or more judges to recuse in a given case. Not too long ago, Mark Kennedy and I voted in a criminal case after two of those judges recused.

Arden: Would you be asked to write an opinion?

Janie: Not unless it came to be a total recusal, requiring a special court.

Arden: Does that ever happen?

Janie: Very, very infrequently. I think it has happened once or twice. But it is not uncommon for a judge to recuse in a particular case. During my time on the Court, it happened not infrequently. A judge is not required to state his reasons for eliminating himself from voting in a case, but it should be for good, valid reasons. It should not be because the case is difficult either personally or politically. Sometimes a judge prefers to be shown "not sitting" when recusal is not warranted. When I was there, that was not unusual.

No Regrets

Arden: Are there any regrets that you have regarding the Court?

Janie: No, not at all.

Arden: So it suited your personality?

Janie: For many reasons. Some of my earliest memories are of being frustrated that I wasn't old enough for people to listen to me. I thought it was because I was so young. However, at a later age, I realized, no, that's not the problem. It's was because I was a girl that they were not listening. And I haven't gotten over my astonishment at that revelation yet! It became an ongoing motivation for me to get into a position where my thoughts were heard and could make a difference. On the Supreme Court, every judge has an equal voice.

Arden: Anything that you might have done differently?

Janie: As a member of the Court, I don't think so. Personally, I should have demanded more from my law clerks and probably should have given them more responsibility; but again, because of the volume of cases we were responsible for, I didn't spend much time on the administrative duties of my office. I was fortunate that most of the time I was there I had competent, experienced secretaries who were much better than I was in managing the work of the clerks.

Many of the justices became quite close to their clerks and most of them relied upon them much more than I did on mine. In retrospect, I regret that. I still hear from some of my former clerks. Many went on to successfully practice law and many have kept in touch with me. I appreciate that.

Arden: You mentioned that a number of justices retired about the same time. Did that make a substantive difference in the performance of the court?

Janie: Well, insofar as an approach to the law or the handling of cases, it made no difference whatsoever. But there was definitely more concern with deciding cases in a timely manner.

It probably appeared that we were taking the Court in a more liberal direction than the Court before us had taken. But there was no question in my mind that we were applying the law as we saw it. I think it was just because in a very short period of time we had an almost total transformation in the make-up of the Court, against a background of a Court that consisted of the same people for 30 years.

Arden: Do you sometimes wish you had made it to the Supreme Court of the United States?

Janie: Of course I do. First of all, it seems to assure longevity. But seriously, it's the most perfect job in the world for a person like me, a person who enjoys the history of the legal system, the evolution of the common law, its duration over time, and the luxury of having as much time as you want to spend on one case with really bright intellectual power to help, and the association with some of the best legal minds in the country.

I can't imagine a better job for my personality, for my talents and interests than that. I can also imagine that it would be totally unsatisfying to many other people. It suits some and not others.

I don't think it's possible to have that kind of working co-existence with colleagues for the long time that the judges do and not come out of it without a very, very high regard for each other. And I think they all do. The judges may vote differently and they don't all agree on everything but historically the judges respect one another's work, and the public retains a high regard for the Court's integrity.

However, I must confess that the Court's decision in *Citizens United* has shaken the confidence that many of us had that politics plays no role in the decision-making process. I think it is laudable for justices to be able to disagree on the law while still retaining amicable relationships among one another.

Arden: Some strange friendships develop. I've heard that most justices seldom see each other on a day-to-day basis.

Janie: I understand that. Isolated work time is a part of the court culture. In my experience, each justice works within his or her individual office, writing and studying opinions with their respective staffs and each spends relatively little time in general meetings with other justices.

I found it to be quite a solitary life, but did not object to that. I loved the job. I loved the law, the majesty of it, the wisdom of the common law, the vision of the founders of this country. To be a participant in the process was a source of real pride to me.

Just Call Me Janie

JANIE SHORES

Vincent Fonde Kilborn, Sr.

Laura, Janie, and James L. Shores, Jr.

Laura's Smith College Graduation

RE-ELECT JUSTICE JANIE SHORES

Experience, Fairness, Integrity

Keep Experienced Leadership On Our Supreme Court

Justice Shores has served as the voice of common sense on Alabama's Supreme Court for 17 years. As Alabama's first woman justice, she has brought national respect to our highest court through her unbiased judicial decisions, experience, knowledge of the law, and efficient running of the business of the court.

Justice Shores has the experience needed to face the pressing issues of today:

- A demonstrated understanding of the important ideals of family life, a history of decisions protecting individual rights and tough views on criminal justice;
- 17 years of implementing and sustaining the standards and practices that have made the Alabama Supreme Court respected throughout the United States.

Keep Alabama's Supreme Court fair and honest.

Vote November 3 for Justice Shores, Supreme Court of Alabama, Place No. 2

Just Call Me Janie

JANIE IS A LEGAL SCHOLAR

There is no higher respect to be paid to Janie Shores than that of her peers—lawyers throughout Alabama who realize Janie's knowledge about law and the infinite ways it works.

To begin with, Janie is an astute lawyer. She was a legal researcher and law clerk to former Supreme Court Justice Robert T. Simpson.

She's an author of numerous articles in legal publications. An editor of authorized instructions to Alabama juries. Member of the Alabama Law Institute.

She served as a staff member on the Alabama Constitutional Revision Commission. And worked ardently for the Judicial Article to the State Constitution, now in effect.

As a law professor at Samford University's Cumberland School of Law, Janie has taken apart our governing laws. Examined them from all sides. Researched countless legal problems and interpretations.

Janie Shores is the kind of legal scholar lawyers throughout the State seek out for advice. The kind who's been invited by the Supreme Court, itself, to work on special matters.

Alabama is fortunate to have such a legal mind as Janie Shores. Janie belongs on Alabama's Supreme Court.

ABOUT JANIE SHORES

South Alabama is an important part of Janie's life.

Born in Georgiana, in 1932, she is the daughter of Mr. and Mrs. John Wesley Ledlow. Growing up in Baldwin County, she was graduated first in her class from Robertsdale High School. And her legal career actually saw its first beginning in Mobile as a legal secretary.

Janie was graduated #1 in her class from the University of Alabama School of Law in Tuscaloosa. She also served as an editor of the *Alabama Law Review*.

After two years of private law practice in Selma, she practiced law in Birmingham for five years. In 1966, Janie Shores joined the faculty at Cumberland School of Law, Samford University, where she is professor of law.

With it all, Janie is a family person. She's the wife of Birmingham attorney, Jim Shores, and the mother of their 10-year-old daughter, Laura.

Re-Election Brochure

Janie with President Jimmy Carter

Janie with Senator
Howell Heflin

JUST CALL ME JANIE

Oscar Adams, Janie Shores, Sam Beatty, Gormon Houston,
Richard 'Red' Jones, Hugh Maddox,
Chief Justice C.C. 'Bo' Torbert, James Faulkner, Reneau Almon

Janie with Hillary Clinton

Justice Janie Shores

Janie Today

Just Call Me Janie

POSTSCRIPT

My thanks to John O'Melveny Woods, Anne Kent Rush, and Arden Schell without whose efforts these conversations would have disappeared into the archives of history.

Janie

Janie Shores' Law Clerks

Doug Ghee
Rick Lyerly
George Kasouf
Holly Wiseman
Belle Stoddard
Tim Morrison
E. J. Saad
Joe Fawal
Heather Lindsay
Leila Hirayama Watson
Greg Shaw
Fred Simpler
Elsie Deutsch Garbrielson
Sophie Truslow
Kathryn Thurman
Charles Haigler
Andrew Allen
Belinda Barnett
Stephen Becker
Patricia Bortz
Terri Bozeman
Sally Broach
Rosemary Buntin
Ronald Dudley
Stan Glascox
Tim Hutchinson
James Ingram
Victor Johnson
Andrew Kaplan
Brian Key
Melissa Math
Bratton Rainey
Sebie Sellers
Rusha Smith
Robert Spense
Michael Stephens
Mike Worel

REFERENCES

For additional photos, reference material, testimonials, and insights from friends and colleagues, please visit the website:

www.JanieShores.com
Or
www.JustCallMeJanie.com

EXPANDED CONTENTS

FOREWORD: VINCENT FONDE KILBORN III
INTERVIEWER'S NOTE: ARDEN SCHELL

SECTION ONE: ROOTS
" *We hold these truths to be self-evident, that all men are created equal, that they are endowed by their Creator with certain unalienable Rights, that among these are Life, Liberty and the Pursuit of Happiness. That to secure these Rights, Governments are instituted among Men, deriving their just powers from the consent of the governed.*"
U. S. Declaration of Independence, 1776

INTERVIEW I - 2/10/2010
FROM POTATOES TO PROFESSOR –PG. 5
PG. 11 – PEARL HARBOR 1941
PG. 12 – POTATO PICKING
PG. 16 – A WOMAN NAMED WILLIE
PG. 18 – LOOKING FOR SPIES
PG. 20 – A BUS TO A NEW LIFE
PG. 21 – JANIE'S SUMMARIES SAVE THE DAY

PG. 23 – A MENTOR RECOGNIZES TALENT
 - *VINCENT F. KILBORN, JR.; JACK EDWARDS; GOLDWATER SWEEP*
PG. 27 – A YOUNG MAN FROM SELMA
 - *BILL ELLZEY*
PG. 28 - BROWN V. BOARD OF EDUCATION
PG. 29 - LAW SCHOOL BEFORE COLLEGE –
 - *CUMBERLAND LAW SCHOOL; CORDELL HULL; ARTHUR WEEKS*
PG. 30 - FIRST FEMALE LAW PROFESSOR IN THE SOUTH
 - *SAMFORD COLLEGE*
PG. 32 - SELMA RESPONDS TO INTEGRATION RULING
PG. 33 - AUTHERINE LUCY MAKES HISTORY 1956
 - *JIM FOLSOM; GEORGE HAWKINS*
PG. 34 - GEORGE WALLACE THE LIBERAL
 - *JOHN PATTERSON; KU KLUX KLAN; GEORGE WALLACE*
PG. 35 - BULL CONNOR RESISTS INTEGRATION
 - *TOM KING*
PG. 35 - A HANDSHAKE SEALS TOM KING'S FATE
 - *ART HANES; WHITE CITIZENS COUNCIL; JIM CLARK*
PG. 36 - MONTGOMERY BUS BOYCOTT
 - *ROSA PARKS; M.L. KING; JOHN KENNEDY; FRANK JOHNSON*
PG. 40 - THE PHILADELPHIA DREXELS
 - *CECIL JACKSON*
PG. 41 - JANIE JOINS THE BAR
PG. 42 - ALABAMA'S FIRST FEMALE LAW PROFESSOR
 - *DEAN LEIGH HARRISON*
PG. 44 - ALL QUALIFIED AND NOWHERE TO WORK
 - *VULCAN MATERIALS; IRA BURLESON; LIBERTY NATIONAL LIFE INSURANCE CO.; JOHN DAVID SNODGRASS; ANNETTE CLARK*
PG. 46 - ENTER JIM SHORES
 - *CHUCK MORGAN; JANIE'S SUMMARIES*
PG. 48 - LAW SCHOOL DAYS
 - *MAX ROGERS; AL RITCHEY; JANIE'S SUMMARIES*

PG. 50 - CAKES & COOKBOOKS BY MORRIS & MILLARD
- *HABITAT FOR HUMANITY; SO. POVERTY LAW CENTER; SAG WALLACE; SPUTNIK*

PG. 53 - "OUT-SEGGED"
- *GEORGE WALLACE; JAMES H. FAULKNER; BALDWIN PRESS; JOHN PATTERSON; PHENIX CITY; LYNDON JOHNSON; CIVIL RIGHTS ACT; BROWN V. BOARD OF EDUCATION*

PG. 54 - JUDGE SIMPSON'S LAW CLERK
- *HOWELL HELFIIN*

PG. 55 - LAURA IS BORN
- *JIM SHORES; TOM KING; BIRMINGHAM NEWS; CHUCK MORGAN; FREEDOM RIDERS*

PG. 57 - CHUCK MORGAN SPEAKS OUT
- *16TH STREET BAPTIST CHURCH BOMBING; DR. A.G. GASTON; ARTHUR SHORES; HUGO BLACK; PAUL JOHNSTON; VIOLA LIUOZZO; ERIC EMBRY; THE NEW YORK TIMES V. SULLIVAN*

PG. 59 - THE CASE OF THE TWO JIMMYS

INTERVIEW II - 2/16/2010
A DOG NAMED DEMOCRAT – PG. 61

PG. 61 - REMEMBRANCE OF FRIENDS PAST
- *FRANCES HART; SHERIFF JIM CLARK; EDMOND PETTUS BRIDGE*

PG. 64 - OUT OF THE FRYING PAN

PG. 65 – BOB AND HELEN VANCE

PG. 67 - DOG DAYS
- *GEORGE WALLACE'S GREAT DANE; DAN T. CARTER*

PG. 69 - HEFLIN FIGHTS FOR CONSTITUTIONAL AMENDMENT
- *LEAGUE OF WOMEN VOTERS*

PG. 71 - WHAT MADE JANIE RUN?
- *AL. SUPREME COURT CAMPAIGN; ANNETTE DODD*

PG. 74 - THE HIGH PRICE OF OFFICE

PG. 75 - REPUBLICAN EFFORT TO ELIMINATE JURY TRIAL
- *KARL ROVE; INSURANCE COMPANIES; TORT REFORM*

JUST CALL ME JANIE

PG. 76 - JURY TRIAL ON TRIAL
- *U.S. CONSTITUTION; BUSH V. GORE; PORNOGRAPHY CASES*

PG. 78 - RULE OF LAW VS. RULE OF PERSONAL OPINION

INTERVIEW III- 11/29/2010
PARENTS, PATRONS, & PREJUDICE – PG. 81
PG. 82 - BANKS & MORTGAGES ARE BAD
PG. 85 - THE MYSTERY OF DISAPPEARING STEVE
PG. 86 – GIRLS DON'T HUNT
- *TRUDY KING; MARCUS KING; UNCLE HOLLIS; RAISING CHICKENS*

PG. 89 – ROBERTSDALE'S ONE UNLISTED NUMBER
- *TIM COOK, CEO OF APPLE*

PG. 89 - MULTI-CULTURAL COUNTRY LIFE
PG. 91 - GRADE SCHOOL EXPECTATIONS
PG. 94 - THE PLEASURE OF TEACHING
PG. 96 - BEING WITH BILL
PG. 97 - MR. ELLZEY'S INTERESTS
- *WHITE CITIZENS COUNCIL*

PG. 101 – DIVORCING SELMA
- *TREATMENT OF DOMESTIC HELP*

PG. 103 – THE INVISIBLE LINE
- *SCHOOLS THAT FEAR BUILT; MONGRELIZATION; MOUNTAIN BROOK; BROWN V. BOARD OF EDUCATION*

PG. 105 – HARDSHIP & HEROES
- *ROSA PARKS; CLIFFORD & VIRGINIA DURR; PAUL JOHNSTON*

PG. 105 – MRS. DURR POWDERS HER NOSE
- *MCCARTHY HEARINGS; GOULD BEECH; MARIE STOKES JEMISON; MONTGOMERY BUS BOYCOTT; VOTER REGISTRATION; FRED GRAY; E.D. NIXON*

PG. 109 – SAG WALLACE
- *CECIL JACKSON; DON PATTERSON; SAG AT THE HOSPITAL*

PG. 110 – KENNEDY IN 1960

PG. 111 - BIRMINGHAM BATTLES
- *TOM KING; DAVID VANN; PEACHES TAYLOR*

PG. 112 - LIBERAL BIRMINGHAM
- *BOB & HELEN VANCE; MR. ARANT; TOM KING; JIM SHORES; VULCAN*

PG. 117 - PHOTOS

SECTION TWO: RIGHTS
"A State Supreme Court's responsibility is to correct errors of lower courts, deciding cases based solely on U.S. law, regardless of the personal politics and preferences of the judges."

USlegal.com

INTERVIEW IV – 12/5/2010
FROM JANIE'S SUMMARIES TO THE SUPREME COURT – PG. 127

PG. 128 – THE CASE FOR RETIREMENT
- *1901 AL. STATE CONSTITUTION REFORM; HOWELL HEFLIN; JIMMY BLOODWORTH; CAMPAIGN FOR AL. SUPREME COURT JUDGE; ERIC EMBRY; ARTHUR GOLDWAITE; BUCKETHEAD FANT*

PG. 132 - THE FAUX FAULKNER
- *JAMES FAULKNER; ARTHUR SHORES; KKK; BULL CONNOR*

PG. 133 - THE ADMIRABLE JUDGE SIMPSON

PG. 136 - SEX & THE SUPREME COURT
- *JUST CALL ME JANIE*

PG. 137 - HER FIRST CAMPAIGN
- *JIMMY BLOODWORTH; JIMMY FAULKNER; RED JONES; ERIC EMBRY; RENEAU ALMON*

PG. 139 – THE SENIORITY FACTOR
- *JOHN DAVID SNODGRASS; RENEAU ALMON; ERIC EMBRY; DR. GASTON; CHRIS MCNAIR; OSCAR ADAMS; JANIE'S SWEARING IN; JUDGE MERRILL; MERRILL DIVISION*

PG. 141 - SELECTING CASES

PG. 142 - A BIRMINGHAM TRADITION BEGINS
- *BIRMINGHAM OFFICE; ARTHUR WEEKS; RED JONES*

Just Call Me Janie

PG. 144 – A CLERK ON THE CLOCK
    - *DOUG GHEE; RICK LYERLY; CLERK TERMS*
PG. 145 - NOBODY SAID IT WAS EASY

INTERVIEW V– 12/12/2010
COFFEE WITH BEAR BRYANT; CAKE WITH MORRIS DEES - PAGE 149
PG. 150 – KILBORN CONNECTIONS
PG. 151 – MISS ROSA GERHARDT
PG. 152 – SCHOOL TIES THAT BIND
    - *MARY JEAN DEAN*
PG. 152 – COMPETITION WITH MAX
    - *CHARLES MCPHERSON AUGUSTIN ROGERS, III*
PG. 153 – LAW REVIEW
PG. 154 – COFFEE WITH BEAR BRYANT
    - *DRUID DRUG STORE; COACH WHITWORTH*
PR. 155 – THE INVISIBLE WOMAN
PG. 157 – LAW SCHOOL FRIENDS
    - *DON PATTERSON; BEN REEVES; MAX ROGERS; RICHARD SHELBY; JOHN DAVID SNODGRASS; ANNETTE CLARK*
PG. 159 – MORRIS & MILLARD MAKE HISTORY
PG. 160 – LIMITED OPPORTUNITIES FOR WOMEN IN LAW
    - *NINA MIGLIONICO; SANDRA DAY O'CONNOR; MRS. DREXEL*
PG. 162 – JEWISH COMMUNITY IN SELMA
    - *HANK & ROSE SANDERS*
PG. 163 – BIG MONEY, LESS JUSTICE, & LITTLE EDUCATION
    - *KARL ROVE*

INTERVIEW VI – 1/11/2011
A JUDGE'S WORK IS NEVER DONE – PG. 167
PG. 167 – AN EMBARRASSMENT OF RACISTS
    - *1901 AL. CONSTITUTION; GOV. ALBERT BREWER; HOWELL HEFLIN*
PG. 168 – HOWELL HEFLIN'S SUCCESS
PG. 169 – CREATING THE COURT OF CIVIL APPEALS

JANIE SHORES

PG. 170 – JUSTICE IS A BLIND DOCKET
PG. 172 – LESS TALK LEADS TO LESS DEEP THOUGHT
PG. 173 – IN JANIE'S OPINIONS
PG. 174 – DRIVING JANIE
PG. 176 – A DAY IN THE LIFE
PG. 178 – CONFERENCE ROOM PROCEDURE
PG. 179 – JANIE'S EFFICIENCY REFORMS
- *GENERAL CONFERENCE; DIVISION CONFERENCE; OPINIONS; CHIEF JUSTICE BO TORBERT; JUSTICE PELHAM MERRILL; JUSTICE HUGH MADDOX*
PG. 182 – SENIORITY IS SERIOUS
PG. 182 – THE MERRILL DIVISION
PG. 183 – FIVE VOTES RULE
PG. 184 – COURT CAST OF CHARACTERS
- *CHIEF JUSTICE HOWELL HEFLIN; PELHAM MERRILL; HUGH MADDOX; JIMMY BLOODWORTH; RICHARD 'RED' JONES; JAMES FAULKNER; ERIC EMBRY; RENEAU ALMON; JANIE SHORES*
PG. 186 – THE 90S CONSERVATIVE SWEEP
- *KARL ROVE*
PG. 187 – NOT RUNNING FOR IMPERSONAL REASONS
- *HOWELL HEFLIN; KARL ROVE; MARK KENNEDY*
PG.189 - PHOTOS

SECTION THREE: REFORMS
"In all criminal prosecutions, the accused shall enjoy the right to a speedy and public trial, by an impartial jury."
U.S. Constitution, Bill of Rights, Amendment VI

INTERVIEW VII – 1/19/2011
JUSTICE IS TRIAL BY JURY – PG. 199
PG. 200 – THE JURY SYSTEM UNDER SIEGE
PG. 203 – A CASE OF EQUAL PROTECTION
- *WOMEN'S LEGAL RIGHTS TO DECIDE*
PG. 205 – COURT RULES SOLELY ON ISSUES PRESENTED

JUST CALL ME JANIE

PG. 206 – LABELING MYSELF
PG. 207 – THE DANGERS OF CURRENT TORT REFORM
PG. 209 – RUNNING LURLEEN WALLACE
PG. 210 – JUDGE MERRILL'S LAST CASE
    - *JACKSON V. CITY OF FLORENCE*
PG. 211 – IT'S BILL CLINTON'S OFFICE CALLING
    - *BERNIE NUSSBAUM; GERALDINE FERRARO; RUTH GINSBERG*

INTERVIEW VIII – 2/2/2011
SHE NEVER LOST A CASE – PG. 213
PG. 215 – BO TORBERT BOOSTS A BUILDING
    - *CHIEF JUSTICE ERNEST 'SONNY' HORNSBY*
PG. 216 – KARL ROVE HELPS ELECT PERRY HOOPER
    - *REPUBLICANS DOMINATE COURT*
PG. 217 – THE LAST DEMOCRAT
    - *CHIEF JUSTICE SUE BELL COBB; ROY MOORE*
PG. 218 – MEDIA COVERAGE FOR ROY MOORE
    - *MOORE CLOSES JANIE & RED JONES' OFFICES; TEN COMMANDMENTS; U.S. DISTRICT JUDGE MYRON THOMPSON*
PG. 219 – ALABAMA THE UNCONSTITUTIONAL
PG. 220 – CAMELOT COURT
    - *HOWELL HEFLIN*
PG. 221 – HIGH COST OF CAMPAIGNS
    - *WALLACE REFUSES TO FILL COURT VACANCIES*
PG. 223 – GOOD GUYS DON'T RUN
PG. 223 – SPECIAL COURTS
PG. 225 – NO REGRETS
PG. 229 - PHOTOS

Books & Other Media

Carter, Dan T.;
    THE POLITICS OF RAGE; Simon & Schuster, 1995.

Elliott Sr., Carl,
    THE COST OF COURAGE, Doubleday, 1992.

Gaillard, Frye;
    ALABAMA'S CIVIL RIGHTS TRAIL, University of Alabama Press, 2010.
    CRADLE OF FREEDOM: Alabama and the Movement that Changed America, University of Alabama Press, 2004.
    GO SOUTH TO FREEDOM, New South Books, 2016.

Jemison, Marie Stokes & Sullivan, Ellen, Eds.,
    AN ALABAMA SCRAPBOOK; Honeysuckle Imprint, 1998.

Morgan Jr., Charles;
    A TIME TO SPEAK, Harper & Row, 1964.

National Public Radio Interview: "A Struggle to Overcome a Legacy of Segregationism"; The Story of Peggy Wallace, George Wallace's daughter, & husband, Mark Kennedy, atty.

Stevenson, Bryan:
    JUST MERCY: A Story of Justice and Redemption, Spiegel & Grau, 2014.

Nevin, David & Bills, Robert E.;
SCHOOLS THAT FEAR BUILT: Segregationist Academies in the South, Acropolis Books, 1976.

Toobin, Jeffrey,
THE NINE: Inside the Secret World of the Supreme Court, Doubleday, New York, 2007.

JANIE SHORES

LETTER FROM THE WHITE HOUSE

THE WHITE HOUSE

Office of the Press Secretary

For Immediate Release January 6, 1995

PRESIDENT (CLINTON) NAMES JANIE SHORES TO STATE JUSTICE INSTITUTE

The President has announced his intent to nominate Justice Janie Ledlow Shores to the State Justice Institute.

Justice Shores of Alabama has been serving as an Associate Justice of the Alabama Supreme Court since 1974, becoming the first woman justice to hold this position. Previously, Justice Shores was a law professor at Cumberland Law School. From 1961 to 1965, she was a member of the legal staff of the Liberty National Life Insurance Company. She was also a law clerk to the late Justice Robert T. Simpson, Associate Justice of the Alabama Supreme Court. Justice Shores received a B.A. from Samford University in Birmingham in 1968, a J.D. from the University of Alabama Law School in 1959 and an LL.M. from the University of Virginia in 1992.

The State Justice Institute is a private, non-profit corporation which provides financial support to projects designed to improve the administration and quality of justice in the State courts. The goals of the Institute are to direct a national program of assistance to ensure that all U.S. citizens have ready access to a fair and effective judicial system; foster coordination and cooperation between the State and Federal judiciaries; serve as a clearing-house and information center for the dissemination of information regarding State judicial systems; and encourage education for judges and support personnel in State court systems.

Just Call Me Janie

Janie Shores

Publisher's Note

I first met Janie Shores at an event where she was volunteering. I exchanged pleasantries, helped her open some wine bottles, and asked her about herself. "Oh, I'm retired," she matter-of-factly replied. I liked her immediately. Unpretentious.

I found out how much so a few moments later.

When I mentioned I had met her, my friends explained that Janie was a retired Alabama Supreme Court Justice, the first woman in the United States to hold that elected position.

"What?" I exclaimed. Weaving back to her station, I confirmed what they had told me. I gave her my card, and suggested that I would like to write a story about her for the newspaper. That was the start of a friendship and journey that has culminated with the publishing of this book.

The more I learn about Janie's life, the more I realize what a truly inspirational and remarkable woman she is, breaking down barriers at every stage of her life, with grace, charm, wit, and humility.

Her noteworthy accomplishments speak for themselves. I hope that after reading this book, the reader will also appreciate her intelligence, sense of humor, and tenacity in remaining true to her sense of justice and right and wrong. She has accomplished an amazing body of work for one lifetime.

Most importantly, this book shows how someone can rise above seemingly limited circumstances and accomplish whatever they put their mind to.

In rereading the final version, I have come to realize how important a book this has turned out to be — helping to define a life and time in history that includes being a champion for racial equality and a strong role model for women and men everywhere.

I also realize how fortunate I am to have met Janie at that event.

John O'Melveny Woods

JANIE SHORES

A "DISSENTING" OPINION
WRITTEN BY JUSTICE JANIE SHORES

In the midst of the thousands of very serious cases Justice Janie Shores heard and wrote about, she never lost her sense of humor. This dissenting opinion shows how she could use her wit to make a point..

Note from Janie: *Hank Williams, born in Alabama, died at age 29 in 1953. He was survived by a wife and son, Hank, Jr. Many years later, a young woman who had been adopted and reared by a Mobile couple filed a lawsuit claiming she was Hank's daughter and thus entitled to a part of his estate. Hank, Jr. disagreed, and this litigation was the result. I believed too much time had passed, and the trial court should have dismissed the case. The majority held otherwise. I submitted the following brief in support of my dissenting position.*

The young plaintiff now calls herself Jett Williams and sings like her dad.

You can't make this stuff up.

****

JUST CALL ME JANIE

Case Number: 07-0269

<u>Catherine Yvonne Stone v. Gulf American Fire and Casualty Co.</u>

Shore, Justice (Dissenting)

HELP ME UNDERSTAND

A little girl prayed at the close of the day
'Cause her daddy had gone far away.
On her little face was a look of despair-
I stood there and listened and I heard the prayer:
My mommy says daddy has brought us to shame,-
I'm never no more to mention his name.
Lord, take me and lead me and hold to my hand-
Oh, Heavenly Father, Help Me Understand.

(Words and Music by Hank Williams)

At the risk of being considered one who has a "Cold, Cold Heart," I respectfully dissent, as I cannot free my doubtful mind about the legal inconsistencies of this opinion. My esteemed colleagues have done "The Alabama Waltz" where all fears and cares are lost to reach the result in this opinion, ignoring all law in existence at each critical time in the appellant's legal journey to share in Hank Williams' songs.

When I consider the facts of this case, "There's a Tear in My Beer" and I'm crying for a child from "A House Without Love" who could have lived in "A Mansion On The Hill."

Bobbie W. Jett heard "Hey Good Lookin', Whatcha Got Cookin'" and was in love. She hopped into the hot-rod Ford, spent the two-dollar bill and went to the spot right over the hill, "Honky Tonkin'" 'round the town.

Hiram "Hank" Williams wooed her with "I Can't Get You Off Of My Mind, when I try I'm just wastin' my time." Soon there was a baby on the way and the refrains of "I'm A Long Gone Daddy" filled the air. Hank went ridin' on the midnight train, taking ev'rything except his ball and chain.

"Why Don't You Love Me like you used to do- How come you treat me like a worn out shoe- My hair's still curly and my eyes are still blue" "I Can't Help It if I'm still in love with you," said Bobbie Jett.

"Hear that lonesome whippoorwill, He sounds too blue to fly- The midnight train is whining low- I'm So Lonesome I Could Cry." (I am, too. Only Almon joins me in dissent.)

Hank's mother Lillian Stone heard Bobbie Jett "Moanin' the Blues," moseying around with her head in her hands singing the "Long Gone Lonesome Blues." She feared that Bobbie would find her a river as cold as ice and go down in it three times but only come up twice.

Mama Stone knew that when the Lord made Hank he made a "Ramblin' Man." Many's the time she'd said, "Your Cheatin' Heart will make you weep- You'll cry and cry- and try to sleep- But sleep won't come- The whole night through- Your Cheatin' Heart- will tell on you."

"Mind Your Own Business," sang Hank, "'Cause if you mind your bus'ness then you won't be mindin' mine." "Now you're lookin' at a man that's gettin' kinda mad- I've had a lot of luck but it's all been bad.- No matter how I struggle and strive- I'll Never Get Out Of This World Alive."

"You Win Again," said Mama Stone. She begged Hank to accept his child. She'd heard him sing "Tonight my head is bowed in sorrow- I can't keep the tears from my eyes- My Son Calls Another Man Daddy- The right to his love I've been denied" and didn't want this to happen again.

"Your head is as wooden as poor old 'Kaw-Liga,'" she said, "I'll take your child and raise it. After that, there's nothing to sing about."

My brothers' attempt to remedy all of this will surely cause a lot of pain.

We can safely say, "There'll Be No Teardrops Tonight."

Acknowledgment

These conversations are a part of a project undertaken by the Senior Lawyers Division of the American Bar Association, known as the Women Trailblazers Project. The collection is now housed at the Library of Congress and at Harvard's Schlesinger Library. In the future with the approval of the Senior Lawyers Division of the ABA, it will be administered by Stanford Law School Robert Crown Law Library.

We are grateful for the vision shown by the Senior Lawyers Division of the ABA that has resulted in the preservation of these histories.

Just Call Me Janie

Janie Shores

www.ingramcontent.com/pod-product-compliance
Lightning Source LLC
Chambersburg PA
CBHW030333230426
43661CB00032B/1393/J